MODERN BALLROOM DANCING

VICTOR SILVESTER

Winner of the World's Dancing Championship, Chairman of the Imperial Society of Teachers of Dancing Incorporated, Leader of the Victor Silvester Ballroom Orchestra which records exclusively on Columbia records and broadcasts regularly for the B.B.C.

Author of:

OLD TIME DANCING
MORE OLD TIME DANCES
SEQUENCE DANCING
THEORY AND TECHNIQUE OF
BALLROOM DANCING

VICTOR SILVESTER

MODERN BALLROOM DANCING

LONDON : HERBERT JENKINS

Published by
Herbert Jenkins Ltd.
3 Duke of York Street,
London, S.W.1.
1952

46th edition, completing 440,360 *copies,* 1953

MADE AND PRINTED IN GREAT BRITAIN BY PURNELL AND SONS, LTD.
PAULTON (SOMERSET) AND LONDON

CONTENTS

PART I

MAINLY FOR BEGINNERS

PART II

FOR THOSE WHO ARE NO LONGER BEGINNERS

ACKNOWLEDGMENTS

I wish to express my thanks and appreciation to Doreen Horn,
Highly Commended Fellow of the Imperial Society of Teachers
of Dancing Incorporated (Ballroom Branch), Principal of the
Mayfair School of Dancing, Luton, Beds., and head assistant at
my Bond Street School for seven years, for the invaluable assistance she has given me in the complete revision of this new
edition.

And to Norman Watts, Fellow of the Imperial Society of
Teachers of Dancing Incorporated (Ballroom Branch) and
Member of the Latin American Branch, Principal of the Mayfair
School of Dancing, Luton, Beds., for drawing all the diagrams.

V.S.

PART I
MAINLY FOR BEGINNERS

CHAPTER I

ON DANCING

BALLROOM dancing is the most popular pastime in the world. There has been no more striking development in social habits than the rise of dancing to universal popularity.

Dancing is a social asset, and for exercise and slimming it is one of the healthiest activities.

In the average ballroom the words "modern ballroom dancing" too often indicate a shuffle round the ballroom in or out of time with the music. Have *you* ever watched couples dancing? Were it possible for them to see themselves, shame alone would prompt them to improve their standard of dancing.

However little you may know about correct methods of dancing, you are sure to be able to pick out of a crowd those who are really enjoying "dancing" and not merely enjoying each other's company or the noise and excitement of the occasion; I refer to those who move with ease and in rhythm with the music. They may not utter a word during an entire dance and yet they are really happy. Maybe they dance very few figures, but those which they perform look neat and simple, not untidy or complicated. I am not referring to professional couples or amateur competition-dancers, who may have spent many years and much money on learning the art of ballroom dancing; I speak of any who take the trouble to move well and dance a few simple basic figures, which, unlike variations, do not change each season.

Few are born dancers, but everyone can dance well enough to become an asset instead of a social menace in a ballroom.

I have often observed that one main idea seems to be to get round the floor in the shortest space of time, regardless of other couples. The object should be to use all available space to the best advantage. In most ballrooms today this means that "Rhythm" or "Crush" dancing should be danced to all Foxtrot tempos. The Quickstep and Slow Foxtrot require more space than the average ballroom affords, but they may be danced by more advanced dancers if, and when, there is enough room on the floor to dance them without discomfort to others.

The Waltz is always popular, whether in Modern, Old Time, or Viennese form. The Modern slow-tempo Waltz in its advanced form takes up rather too much space for small rooms, but the simple figures are quite suitable for any size of ballroom.

The Tango is a dance that causes panic in the mind of the novice, a fact which is a source of amazement to me. The simple figures of this dance are really easier to execute than those of any other dance, and I am firmly of the opinion that if dance bands played more Tangos the dancing public would soon take the floor for them as readily as for the more English rhythms.

So far I have only mentioned standardised dances in the English style, but we must not forget the Rumba and Samba, which are gaining in popularity now that many bands are playing them as part of their repertoire, and some bands even specialising exclusively in these fascinating rhythms.

Sequence and Old Time dances have their following, though they are mostly made up of fairly simple figures, and are easier to learn than the Modern style, because they are often made up of sets of figures repeated to sixteen or thirty-two bars of music, whereas in Modern dances the amalgamation of the figures is largely left to individual dancing couples. These can only look attractive when performed correctly and gracefully.

The English style of ballroom dancing has been copied and taught by practically every good dance teacher throughout the world because it is universally acclaimed as the best. This book will guide you along the right lines to acquiring it.

In the following pages of Part I I have selected dances from the Modern group which are suitable for beginners, bearing in mind that the "social" dancer does not need to learn a detailed technique. I have endeavoured to give some helpful hints which I have found most useful when teaching beginners; these will be of more value to them than detailed descriptions.

I have chosen a very simple syllabus of figures for each dance selected; from experience I have found these figures completely adequate for the average dancer who does not aim at becoming a past-master, but just wishes to learn enough to ensure that his dancing is correct and suitable for any size of ballroom. These figures are also an excellent basis for the more ambitious beginner who, having mastered Part I, can *then* proceed to learn more advanced figures and dances, such as the Quickstep and Slow Foxtrot, and delve deeper into the technicalities in Part II.

The contents of Part I will be found invaluable to teachers of beginners for use in private lessons, also in large or small classes of pupils, youth centres and all types of schools. The figures described are suitable for pupils of all ages.

Finally, it is obviously essential to have suitable music for the proper execution of the dances described. My Ballroom Orchestra, playing in strict tempo, has made many gramophone records for Columbia exclusively for dancing. They may be obtained from any record dealer, and new ones are issued each month.

CHAPTER II
OF PRIME IMPORTANCE

The Hold. Many gentlemen hold their partners at distances up to two feet from them, making it very difficult for the lady to follow the figures. The only dances dealt with in this book in which an open hold may be adopted are the Samba or the Rumba, and then only in certain figures.

The correct hold for each dance is described at the beginning of the chapter dealing with the figures for that dance, but some general points should be noted. If the lady is held close to her partner, and he places his right hand firmly on her back, it will be much easier for him to lead her into the various figures and it will give her much more confidence in following him.

Balance. Golden rules to remember are: when moving forward, keep the feet in a straight line; do not try to avoid your partner's feet by trying to walk outside them; when moving backward, keep the feet in line too—imagine you are "walking the dotted line".

Good balance is really a matter of practise in correct walking. When you are walking in the street, you do not push your feet out in front and allow your body to follow. The same applies in dancing: carry your weight gradually forward with the moving foot. When moving backward, step back onto the toes, bringing the weight gradually back with the forward foot before taking the next step. A more detailed description of walking steps is given for each dance.

The Head. Many dancers do not realise the great importance of the head positions for both partners. Too many couples dance looking at the floor, little realising the effect which this has on their appearance, and also its serious effect on the position of the body, which gives rise to further faults. Keep the head up, chin naturally held in; a good idea is to keep the eyes at their natural level and not to look below that level. The gentleman's head should be turned very slightly leftward, so that he can see over the lady's right shoulder. The lady's head should be poised so that she looks over the gentleman's right shoulder.

The Body. Too many dancers either look stiff or uncontrolled. Those who look too stiff are keeping their muscles taut instead of holding the body in a natural, erect position, without raising the shoulders or pushing from the chest: an appearance of stiffness is usually due to this habit. Those who appear uncontrolled hold their arms loosely drooping at their sides, shoulders sagging, and stomach muscles flabby. The arms should be held up, but without raising the shoulders. Ladies should pay particular attention that they do not hang on their partner, or become heavy by allowing their arms to droop, or by gripping him like a vice. It is a very good idea to think of the stomach muscles as the central point of control of the whole body.

The Legs. Faults that apply to the body apply also to the legs; that is to say, over-stiffness or lack of control. The legs should move freely from the hips, and a natural bracing and relaxing should be used in conjunction with each step. In all English-style dances, the knees, generally speaking, are at their straightest at the full extent of a stride, and relax very slightly as the full weight is taken onto the foot.

The Feet. Points applying to the feet have already been mentioned with reference to balance; that is, keep the feet straight, and do not turn them out or in too much—rather the latter than the former. Out-turned toes are an all too common fault amongst pupils; to correct this is very simple—practise walking properly in the street. If you walk correctly there, you will dance a hundred per cent better, and it will seem *so* much easier. Try to feel your feet brush past each other on all forward and backward steps.

Use of the ankles is very important: when you have reached the full extent of a stride forward, make sure that you have the ankle of the back foot stretched and that only the toes are on the floor, not the ball of the foot as well, before you move on to the next movement of the back foot. The same rule applies when you move backward: see that you step out onto the toes, not just as far as the ball of the foot, before you move the front foot into its next position.

Leading. Quite a number of gentlemen who learn to dance reasonably well as far as the figures, etc., are concerned, find that their partners still complain: "He does not lead me." The task of leading the lady cannot be accomplished until the gentleman has mastered the pattern of the figures; up to this point he is much too preoccupied with his own troubles to worry about leading. Having mastered both the pattern and the amalgamation of the figures to a reasonable standard, the gentleman should then consider very carefully the leading of his partner so that she will follow him with confidence and not have to make wild guesses as to what is coming next. On the other hand, the gentleman should never be led into a figure by his partner anticipating what he is going to do and pulling him into it.

A gentleman must take his steps, in whatever direction they are to go, deliberately, and not half-heartedly. Even if they are incorrect, it is better to do the job thoroughly than to "dither". At least the lady will be more likely to follow you and you are not so likely to fall over each other. She may not even realise that you did something wrong, so long as you lead well. She may think it is a new figure she has not learnt.

Apart from the movement of the legs and body into the various positions, indicating to the lady the direction of each step, the gentleman should use his right hand to lead the lady in all dances except the Samba, Rumba and other dances where both hands are often used. The general rules for gentlemen to remember about the use of the right hand for leading are: if you want your partner to keep in the normal dancing position, almost square in front of you, keep the right hand naturally curved onto her back with even pressure along the hand; if you wish the lady to step outside you, use slight pressure of the fingers of the right hand; if you wish to turn the lady into what is known as Promenade Position (that is, any figure, or part of a figure, where the couple open out fanwise and only the gentleman's right side is in contact with the lady's left side), you should turn the lady by using pressure of the base of the right hand; when you wish her to turn to face you again, you repeat the pressure of the fingers of the right hand.

The Music. Time, tempo and rhythm are dealt with for individual dances in the pages dealing with each dance. However, here are some general hints to those who find the musical side of dancing difficult to follow. Listen to the music before you move off with your partner. It is always a good thing to count to yourself at least one bar of the music before you start, then get ready on the last beat of the bar, making quite sure you are not standing with your weight on the foot you are about to move (this will help your partner to know which foot you are going to start with), and move off so that your first step coincides with the first beat of the next bar. There is no standardised ruling as to which foot to begin with for Modern dances. It is optional, and so long as the gentleman gives a clear indication to his partner, by taking his weight onto the non-moving foot first, it is immaterial whether he starts with the left or the right foot, and may be varied according to the figures he intends to dance first.

If you have difficulty in following the beats of the bar, get someone to count them for you to the music, and practise counting them out loud, or clap them, until you become familiar with them and can keep in time without having to think about it. Dancing out of time with the music is quite a common sight, and usually the offenders are quite oblivious of the fact. People say they cannot hear the beats, but this is usually because their ears have not had any musical training; with a little practice, keeping time soon becomes automatic.

Ballroom Etiquette. It is the gentleman's privilege to ask a lady to dance unless the dance is announced as "Ladies' privilege". A gentleman may receive a refusal simply because of a poor method of address. It is not necessary to use excessive formality nowadays, but reasonable courtesy should be observed. A suitable form of address is (to a stranger) "Would you care to dance?" or "May I have this dance?" If the partner is known, the gentleman may simply say "Shall we dance?"

Once upon the floor, remember that other couples are also there. Avoid a collision, if possible, by taking shorter steps or altering your line of dance. If a collision does occur always apologise to the other couple, even if it was not your fault. When the dance finishes, do not forget to show your appreciation of the band's efforts by clapping. If it is not a very good band, they are probably doing their best, and a little appreciation may encourage them to do better. If after a dance with a stranger you do not wish to sit out with her, always take her back to her seat or to her friends. At the end of a dance both lady and gentleman should, of course, thank each other.

THE POSITIONS OF THE FEET IN RELATION TO THE BALLROOM

(Remember that you dance anti-clockwise round the ballroom)

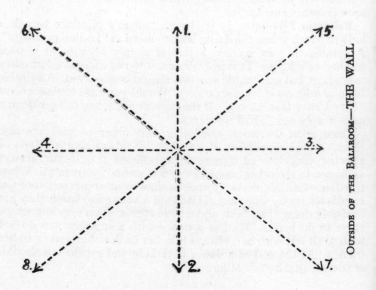

OUTSIDE OF THE BALLROOM—THE WALL

POSITIONS OF THE FEET *(Indicated by arrows)*

1. Facing L.O.D.   counterpart Backing L.O.D.
2. Backing L.O.D.   „   Facing L.O.D.
3. Facing wall.   „   Backing wall.
4. Facing centre.   „   Backing centre.
5. Facing diag. to wall.   „   Backing diag. to wall.
6. Facing diag. to centre.   „   Backing diag. to centre.
7. Facing diag. to wall against L.O.D.   „   Backing diag. to wall against L.O.D.
8. Facing diag. to centre against L.O.D.   „   Backing diag. to centre against L.O.D.

TERMS USED IN DESCRIBING THE DIRECTION OF STEPS

(Remember that you dance anti-clockwise round the ballroom)

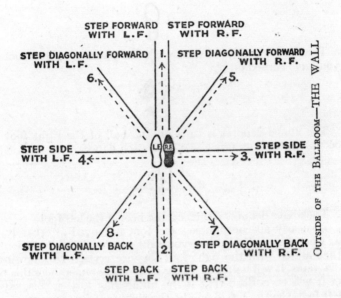

DIRECTIONS OF STEPS (*Indicated by arrows*)

1. Along L.O.D.
2. Against L.O.D.
3. To wall.
4. To centre.
5. Diag. to wall.
6. Diag. to centre.
7. Diag. to wall against L.O.D.
8. Diag. to centre against L.O.D.

HOW TO READ THE DIAGRAMS

In the diagrams the right foot is illustrated thus—

and the left foot—

The dotted outline of the foot is the position of that foot after you have turned on it.

The above denotes a turn on the ball of the right foot as it occurs in the diagrams given with each dance.

The above denotes a turn on the heel of the left foot.

In nearly all the figures each foot is moved alternately, just as when you walk; that is, you take a step with the left foot and then a step with the right foot (or vice versa). In following the diagrams, it will help the reader if he or she remembers this point, or it will be noticed that if the numbering 1, 3, 5, 7 is, say, the left foot, then 2, 4, 6, 8 will be the right foot (or vice versa).

You will find the diagrams easier to follow if you always face the direction in which the toes are pointing. As you turn, turn the diagram as well.

Let your feet follow along the lines in which the arrows are pointing.

The diagrams are not intended to be mathematically exact, but merely to show the pattern made in the different figures. The left side of the page on which each diagram is drawn represents the middle of the ballroom, whilst the right side of the page represents the outside—the wall. The top of the page is equivalent to the line of dance. From this the reader will be able to understand which way he or she should be facing on each step.

EXPLANATIONS OF ABBREVIATIONS USED IN DIAGRAMS AND DESCRIPTIONS OF FIGURES

S.—A slow step.

Q.—A quick step.

R.—Right.

L.—Left.

R.F.—Right foot.

L.F.—Left foot.

Diag.—Diagonally.

L.O.D.—The line of dance. (This means the direction that one takes when dancing round a ballroom. Anti-clockwise.)

C.B.M.—Contrary body movement.

C.B.M.P.—Contrary body movement position.

P.P.—Promenade position. A position similar to that of the Promenade in the Tango, in which the partners open out fanwise to each other, the lady's left hip remaining in contact with the gentleman's right hip.

F.A.P.—Fall away position. This is the Promenade Position in which the couple travel backwards.

Fig.—Figure.

Natural Turn.—Right-handed turn.

Reverse Turn.—Left-handed turn.

O.P.—Outside partner.

P.O.—Partner outside.

H.—Heel.

T.—Toe.

B.—Ball of foot.

CHAPTER III

SLOW AND QUICK RHYTHM DANCING

SOME GENERAL NOTES

THESE two dances are the "Crush" or crowded ballroom form of Slow Foxtrot and Quickstep. "Rhythm" dancing can be danced to any tempo of 4/4 music (four beats in a bar); Slow Foxtrot and Quickstep require a more strict tempo to enable them to be danced in comfort.

Quick Rhythm would be danced to any tempo faster than about forty bars per minute, Slow Rhythm to any tempo slower than forty bars per minute. The accented beats in 4/4 music are the first and third, and the beginner will soon learn to pick out the beats with a little practice.

To make the figures easier to learn, teachers substitute the use of "slows" and "quicks" in place of musical beats, and the pupil has only to remember that "slow"=two beats and "quick"= one beat. One "slow"=two "quicks", and vice versa. I have found with some pupils that even if they say "slow" they are still inclined to take the step at the speed of a "quick"; it is a good idea for a beginner who has this fault to say "slowly" instead of just "slow"; it takes him longer to say, and will thus slow him down a little.

The hold is the same for Quick and Slow Rhythm. The gentleman places his right hand just under the lady's left shoulderblade (a little further round her back, if it is very crowded in the ballroom), with the fingers close together and the hand curved naturally onto her back. The left arm is raised so that his hand is a little above his shoulder level, with the forearm curved at the elbow, so as to appear natural and comfortable. He holds the lady's right hand in his left hand, palm to palm, thumbs crossed. Both elbows should be raised slightly, but without raising the shoulders. His partner should be held as squarely in front of him as possible, though if the room is very crowded and he holds his right hand a little further round the lady she will tend to be a little more towards his right side. The lady raises her right arm to the level of her partner's left arm and places her right hand in his left, as described above. She places her left hand lightly on the gentleman's right upper arm without spreading the fingers,

Photo by Tunbridge

THE HOLD

For Lady and Gentleman

Photo by Tunbridge

THE TANGO HOLD

and keeps her elbows up a little so as not to hang, or weigh down his arm.

All "slow" steps forward and backward are danced like walking steps, and it is an excellent exercise for a beginner to practise correct walking steps before learning the figures, which will also improve balance. It is advisable to practise "walks" even after the figures have been mastered.

The walk forward is based on a natural walking movement—the only difference being that the feet skim lightly along the floor instead of being lifted for each step. The moving foot is pushed forward first with the ball of the foot skimming the floor, going on to the heel as it passes the toes of the other foot; at this point the back heel begins to leave the floor. Continue to the extent of the stride on the heel of the moving foot, gradually releasing the back foot to the ball and then to the toes. At the end of the stride, lower the front toes to the floor, drawing the back foot up from the toes to the ball of the foot, ready for the next walk. Remember to keep the feet in a straight line, neither turned in nor out. For Slow Rhythm, the length of stride can be taken as in a natural walk; but if the room is very crowded, it should be shorter. For Quick Rhythm, the stride should be short—very short when the music is rather quicker than a normal tempo.

The walk backward is also based on the natural movement. The moving foot goes back onto the ball of the foot and then onto the toes, going gradually to the ball again as the front foot is brought back with pressure on the heel, with the toes slightly raised from the floor, until it reaches the back foot, when the toes are lowered, so that the foot is then flat. At this point, and not before, the heel of the back foot reaches the floor. The length of stride should be adapted as for the forward walk.

Each walking step is counted "slow" and takes up two beats of music, so that two walks would take up one bar of music, that is, "slow", "slow"=1,2, 3,4 (one bar).

Note. All steps taken in a sideways direction are taken onto the ball of the foot, and then the heel is lowered, as the whole weight is taken onto the foot.

DIFFERENCES BETWEEN SLOW AND QUICK RHYTHM DANCING

(1) All the figures described for Slow Rhythm may be danced in Quick Rhythm except the Side Step, which is different for each tempo. The Slow Rhythm Side Step is counted as six "quicks" and is therefore not so well suited to Quick Rhythm, as it is rather a rush to get it in at the faster speed. The only other

figure which varies is the Twinkle. The timing is changed for Quick Rhythm, all "slow" timing being much more attractive if applied to the quicker music.

(2) On closing steps in Slow Rhythm, the feet are brought close together. In Quick Rhythm, on the closing steps which occur on a "quick" count, the feet are not brought close together but are only nearly closed; but when a close occurs on a "slow" count in Quick Rhythm, the feet are closed right together.

(3) The steps are usually taken slightly longer for Slow Rhythm than Quick Rhythm.

Body Sway in Rhythm Dancing. This should not be attempted by beginners until they have achieved a reasonable standard of execution of the figures, but body sway will give style and added softness to the various movements if applied thus:

When a step is taken with the right foot, sway slightly from the hips the towards the right; when a step is taken with the left foot, sway slightly from the hips towards the left. Briefly, sway slightly towards the foot you are stepping with.

Quarter Turns

GENTLEMAN

Begin facing diag. to wall.

1. Forward R.F.		s.
2. Side L.F.	} Make ¼ turn to R.	Q.
3. Close R.F. to L.F.		Q.
4. Side L.F. (slightly back)		s.
5. Back R.F.		s.
6. Side L.F.	} Make ¼ turn to L.	Q.
7. Close R.F. to L.F.		Q.
8. Forward L.F.		s.

Finish facing diag. to wall.

LADY

Begin backing diag. to wall.

1. Back L.F.		s.
2. Side R.F.	} Make ¼ turn to R.	Q.
3. Close L.F. to R.F.		Q.
4. Diag. forward R.F.		s.
5. Forward L.F.		s.
6. Side R.F.	} Make ¼ turn to L.	Q.
7. Close L.F. to R.F.		Q.
8. Back R.F.		s.

Finish backing diag. to wall.

This fig. may be preceded by:
(1) The Quarter Turns.
(2) The Natural Pivot Turn.
(3) A walk on the L.F.

This fig. may be followed by:
(1) The Quarter Turns.
(2) The Natural Pivot Turn.
(3) The Reverse Pivot Turn, making the last step of the Quarter Turns the first step of the Reverse Pivot Turn.
(4) The Reverse Pivot and Rotary Chassé.

Natural Pivot Turn

GENTLEMAN

Begin facing diag. to wall.
1. Forward R.F.   S.
2. Side L.F.   ⎫ Make ¼ turn to R.   Q.
3. Close R.F. to L.F. ⎭   Q.
4. Back L.F.   S.

Repeat these four steps three times so as to make a complete turn to R. and finish facing diag. to wall. If used at a corner repeat the four steps twice, making ¾ turn to R.

LADY

Begin backing diag. to wall.
1. Back L.F.   S.
2. Side R.F.   ⎫ Make ¼ turn to R.   Q.
3. Close L.F. to R.F. ⎭   Q.
4. Forward R.F.   S.

Repeat these four steps three times so as to make a complete turn to R. and finish backing diag. to wall. If used at a corner repeat the four steps twice, making ¾ turn to R.

This fig. may be preceded by:
(1) The Quarter Turns.
(2) A walk on the L.F.

This fig. may be followed by:
(1) The Quarter Turns.

Reverse Pivot Turn

GENTLEMAN

Begin facing diag. to wall.
1. Forward L.F.   S.
2. Back onto R.F.   ⎫ Make ¼ turn to L.   S.
3. Side L.F.   ⎭   Q.
4. Close R.F. to L.F.   Q.

Repeat these four steps three times so as to make a complete turn to L. and finish facing diag. to wall.

Reverse Pivot Turn

LADY

Begin backing diag. to wall.

1. Back R.F.		s.
2. Forward onto L.F. } Make ¼ turn to L.		s.
3. Side R.F.		Q.
4. Close L.F. to R.F.		Q.

Repeat these four steps three times so as to make a complete turn to L. and finish backing diag. to wall.

This fig. may be preceded by:
(1) Seven steps of the Quarter Turns.
(2) A Rotary Chassé.

This fig. may be followed by:
(1) A walk on the L.F.
(2) A Rotary Chassé after the first two steps of the Reverse Pivot Turn when it has been danced in full once.

Rotary Chassé from Reverse Pivot Turn

GENTLEMAN

Begin facing diag. to wall.

1. ⎫	s.
2. ⎟ Dance the Reverse Pivot Turn,	s.
3. ⎬ making ¼ turn to L.	Q.
4. ⎭	Q.
5. Forward L.F.	s.
6. Back onto R.F.	s.
7. Side L.F.	Q.
8. Close R.F. to L.F.	Q.
9. Side L.F. Make ¾ turn to L. to complete	Q.
10. Close R.F. to L.F. the whole turn.	Q.
11. Side L.F.	Q.
12. Close R.F. to L.F.	Q.

Finish facing diag. to wall.

LADY

Begin backing diag. to wall.

1. ⎫	s.
2. ⎟ Dance the Reverse Pivot Turn,	s.
3. ⎬ making ¼ turn to L.	Q.
4. ⎭	Q.
5. Back R.F.	s.

6. Forward onto L.F.	S.
7. Side R.F.	Q.
8. Close L.F. to R.F.	Q.
9. Side R.F.	Q.
10. Close L.F. to R.F.	Q.
11. Side R.F.	Q.
12. Close L.F. to R.F.	Q.

Make ¾ turn to L. to complete the whole turn.

Finish backing diag. to wall.

This fig. may be preceded by:
(1) Seven steps of the Quarter Turns.
(2) The Reverse Pivot Turn.

This fig. may be followed by:
(1) A walk on the L.F.
(2) The Reverse Pivot Turn.

Back Corté

GENTLEMAN

Begin backing L.O.D.

1. Back R.F.	S.
2. Side L.F.	Q.
3. Close R.F. to L.F.	Q.
4. Back L.F.	S.

Finish backing L.O.D.

LADY

Begin facing L.O.D.

1. Forward L.F.	S.
2. Side R.F.	Q.
3. Close L.F. to R.F.	Q.
4. Forward R.F.	S.

Finish facing L.O.D.

This fig. may be preceded by:
(1) The first four steps of the Quarter Turns overturned so as to back L.O.D.
(2) The Double Chassé Back Corté.
(3) The first four steps of the Natural Pivot Turn.
(4) The Twinkle, making the last step of the Twinkle the first step of the Back Corté.
(5) The Back Corté.

This fig. may be followed by:
(1) The Back Corté (repeated).
(2) The Twinkle.
(3) The last four steps of the Quarter Turns.
(4) The Double Chassé Back Corté.

Double Chassé Back Corté

GENTLEMAN

Begin backing L.O.D.

1. Back R.F.	S.
2. Side L.F.	Q.
3. Close R.F. to L.F.	Q.
4. Side L.F.	Q.
5. Close R.F. to L.F.	Q.
6. Back L.F.	S.

Finish backing L.O.D.

LADY

Begin facing L.O.D.

1. Forward L.F.	S.
2. Side R.F.	Q.
3. Close L.F. to R.F.	Q.
4. Side R.F.	Q.
5. Close L.F. to R.F.	Q.
6. Forward R.F.	S.

Finish facing L.O.D.

This fig. may be preceded by:
(1) The first four steps of the Quarter Turns overturned so as to back L.O.D.
(2) The Back Corté.
(3) The first four steps of the Natural Pivot Turn.
(4) The Double Chassé Back Corté.
(5) The Twinkle, making the last step of the Twinkle the first step of the Double Chassé Back Corté.

This fig. may be followed by:
(1) The Back Corté.
(2) The Twinkle.
(3) The last four steps of the Quarter Turns.
(4) The Double Chassé Back Corté.

Chassé Reverse Turn

GENTLEMAN

Begin facing L.O.D.

1. Forward L.F.		S.
2. Side R.F.	} Make ½ turn to L.	Q.
3. Close L.F. to R.F.		Q.
4. Back R.F.		S.
5. Side L.F.	} Make ⅜ turn to L.	Q.
6. Close R.F. to L.F.		Q.
7. Forward L.F.		S.

Finish facing diag. to wall.

Chassé Reverse Turn

LADY

Begin backing L.O.D.
1. Back R.F.	s.
2. Side L.F.	Q.
3. Close R.F. to L.F. } Make ½ turn to L.	Q.
4. Forward L.F.	s.
5. Side R.F.	Q
6. Close L.F. to R.F. } Make ⅜ turn to L.	Q.
7. Back R.F.	s.

Finish backing diag. to wall.

This fig. may be preceded by:
(1) The Quarter Turns, making the last step the first step of the Chassé Reverse Turn, but having turned on steps 6 and 7 of the Quarter Turns to face L.O.D. (⅜ turn instead of ¼).

This fig. may be followed by:
(1) The Quarter Turns.
(2) The Natural Pivot Turn.
(3) Five steps of the Quarter Turns into side step.
(4) Four steps of the Quarter Turns into the Back Corté, Back Corté and Twinkle, or Double Chassé Back Corté.

Six Quick Side Step (Slow Rhythm only)

GENTLEMAN

Begin sideways on to L.O.D., toes pointing diag. to wall (P.P.).
1. Side L.F.	Q.
2. Close R.F. to L.F.	Q.
3. Side L.F.	Q.
4. Close R.F. to L.F. without transferring weight onto it.	Q.
5. Side R.F.	Q.
6. Close L.F. to R.F. without transferring weight onto it.	Q.

Finish facing in commencing position.

LADY

Begin sideways on to L.O.D., toes pointing diag. to centre (P.P.).
1. Side R.F.	Q.
2. Close L.F. to R.F.	Q.
3. Side R.F.	Q.
4. Close L.F. to R.F. without transferring weight onto it.	Q.
5. Side L.F.	Q.
6. Close R.F. to L.F. without transferring weight onto it.	Q.

Finish facing in commencing position.

This fig. may be preceded by:
(1) The first five steps of the Quarter Turns.
(2) The Six Quick Side Step.

This fig. may be followed by:
(1) The last three steps of the Quarter Turns.
(2) The Six Quick Side Step repeated once or twice.

Note.—When the gentleman dances the Quarter Turns into the Side Step (from the fifth step of the Quarter Turns) he must open his partner to P.P. When following the Side Step with 6, 7, 8 of the Quarter Turns he must turn her square to him again. (See notes on leading, page 13.)

The Twinkle (Slow Rhythm)

GENTLEMAN

Begin backing L.O.D., having danced the Back Corté.
1. Forward onto R.F.   Q.
2. Close L.F. to R.F.   Q.
3. Back R.F.   S.
Finish backing L.O.D.

LADY

Begin facing L.O.D., having danced the Back Corté.
1. Back onto L.F.   Q.
2. Close R.F. to L.F.   Q.
3. Forward L.F.   S.
Finish facing L.O.D.

This fig. may be preceded by:
(1) The Back Corté.
(2) The Double Chassé Back Corté.

This fig. may be followed by:
(1) The Back Corté, making the last step of the Twinkle the first step of the Back Corté.
(2) The last three steps of the Quarter Turns.
(3) The Double Chassé Back Corté, making the last step of the Twinkle the first step of the Double Chassé Back Corté.

The Twinkle (Quick Rhythm)

GENTLEMAN

Begin backing L.O.D., having danced the Back Corté.

1. Forward onto R.F.		s.
2. Close L.F. to R.F.		s.
3. Back R.F.		s.

Finish backing L.O.D.

Note alteration of timing from Slow Rhythm.

LADY

Begin facing L.O.D., having danced the Back Corté.

1. Back onto L.F.		s.
2. Close R.F. to L.F.		s.
3. Forward L.F.		s.

Finish facing L.O.D.

Note alteration of timing from Slow Rhythm.

This fig. may be preceded by:

(1) The Back Corté.
(2) The Double Chassé Back Corté.

This fig. may be followed by:

(1) The Back Corté.
(2) The last three steps of the Quarter Turns.
(3) The Double Chassé Back Corté.

> *Note* 1 and 3. The last step of the Twinkle will be the first step of the following fig.

Side Step (Quick Rhythm)

GENTLEMAN

Begin sideways on to L.O.D., toes pointing diag. to wall (P.P.).

1. Side L.F.		Q.
2. Half close R.F. to L.F.		Q.
3. Side L.F.		s.
4. Close R.F. to L.F.		s.

Finish facing in commencing position.

Side Step (Quick Rhythm)

LADY

Begin sideways on to L.O.D., toes pointing diag. to centre (P.P.).
1. Side R.F.   Q.
2. Half close L.F. to R.F.   Q.
3. Side R.F.   s.
4. Close L.F. to R.F.   s.
Finish facing in commencing position.

This fig. may be preceded by:
(1) The first five steps of the Quarter Turns.
(2) The Side Step.

This fig. may be followed by:
(1) The last three steps of the Quarter Turns.
(2) The Side Step (repeated once or twice).

Note.—When the gentleman dances the Quarter Turns into the Side Step from the fifth step, he must open his partner to P.P. When the gentleman follows the Side Step with 6, 7 and 8 of the Quarter Turns he must turn his partner square again. (See notes on Leading, page 13.)

This Side Step may also be danced to Slow Rhythm, but the Six Quick Side Step is to be preferred.

Chapter IV

THE WALTZ

Some General Notes

THE modern Waltz can be danced in any ballroom and the figures described can be adapted either for a crowded ballroom or a spacious one. If a ballroom is small or crowded, all the steps are taken very short and without any rise to the toes. If the ballroom is large and not crowded, *all* the steps should be long, and a gradual rise to the toes should be started at the end of the first beat and carried out to the end of the third beat of each bar of music, except where otherwise mentioned in the descriptions of the figures. At the end of the third beat, lower to the normal position by lowering the heel of the foot which is carrying the weight.

The hold is the same as that described for Slow and Quick Rhythm on page 20.

Each step in the figures described takes one beat of the music, the time of the Waltz music is $\frac{3}{4}$ (three beats to the bar). The speed of the Modern Waltz is about thirty-two to thirty-four bars per minute and the accent is on the first beat. There will be no "slows" and "quicks" for beginners to worry about; they need only count in threes, but each count must be even, otherwise the steps will be hurried and the correct timing lost. More dancers get out of time in the Waltz than in any other dance, and it is advisable for a beginner to pay special attention to counting the waltz beats carefully before commencing the dance figures.

It will be seen from the description of the Natural Turn, Right Closed Change, Reverse Turn, and Left Closed Change that the steps in the turns have been numbered 1,2,3 4,5,6; and the Changes 7,8,9. For beginners I have always found it easier if they count the numbers of the steps to themselves 1,2,3 4,5,6 7,8,9 rather than the musical timing, 1,2,3 1,2,3 1,2,3, for the turns and changes. They seem to get muddled with the pattern if they keep repeating the count 1,2,3, but by counting from 1 to 9 they remember when to turn and when to remain facing the same way. In the other figures, also, beginners will find this method helps them to know where a figure begins and ends.

31

When the figures have been mastered and there is plenty of room to "step out" in the Waltz, a slight sway should be introduced not only to soften the look of the figures but also to assist the turns. The sway is unlike that used in Slow and Quick Rhythm in that it is retained to right or left for two beats of music in most figures. The general rule is: If you step with the right foot forward or backward on 1, you sway towards the right for 2 and 3; if you step with the left foot forward or backward on 1, you sway towards the left for 2 and 3. There is one exception in the figures described—there is no sway on 4,5,6 in the Natural Spin Turn.

Other figures and the standard variations will be found in the appropriate chapter in Part II of this book.

Natural Turn (Right Turn)

GENTLEMAN

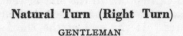

Begin facing diag. to wall.   *Music timing*

1. Forward R.F.	} Turning to R.	1
2. Side L.F.	to back L.O.D.	2 } 1 bar
3. Close R.F. to L.F.		3
4. Back L.F.	} Turning to R.	1
5. Side R.F.		2 } 1 bar
6. Close L.F. to R.F.		3

Finish facing diag. to centre.

This fig. may be preceded by:
(1) The Left Closed Change.
(2) The Reverse Corté.

This fig. may be followed by:
(1) The Right Closed Change.

Advanced Technique of the above Figure

(Not required by the beginner)

Amount of turn: Make ¼ turn to R. between 1 and 2; make ⅛ turn to R. between 2 and 3; make ⅜ turn to R. between 4 and 5.
Footwork: 1. H.T.   2. T.   3. T.H.   4. T.H.   5. T.   6. T.H.
Contrary body movement: Used on 1 and 4.
Body sway: Sway to R. on 2 and 3; sway to L. on 5 and 6.

Right Closed Change

GENTLEMAN

Begin facing diag. to centre.

		Music timing	
7. Forward R.F.	⎫	1	⎫
8. Side L.F.	⎬ No turn.	2	⎬ 1 bar
9. Close R.F. to L.F.	⎭	3	⎭

Finish facing diag. to centre.

This fig. may be preceded by:
(1) The Natural Turn.

This fig. may be followed by:
(1) The Reverse Turn.
(2) 1, 2 and 3 of the Reverse Turn into the Reverse Corté.

Advanced Technique of the above Figure
    (Not required by the beginner)

Amount of turn: Nil.
Footwork: 1. H.T.   2. T.   3. T.H.
Contrary body movement:
    Used on 1 (slightly).
Body sway: Sway to R. on 2 and 3.

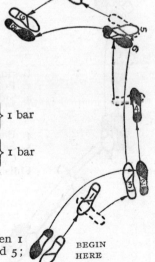

Natural Turn (Right Turn)

LADY

Begin backing diag. to wall.

		Music timing	
1. Back L.F.	⎫	1	⎫
2. Side R.F.	⎬ Turning to R. to face L.O.D.	2	⎬ 1 bar
3. Close L.F. to R.F.	⎭	3	⎭
4. Forward R.F.	⎫	1	⎫
5. Side L.F.	⎬ Turning to R.	2	⎬ 1 bar
6. Close R.F. to L.F.	⎭	3	⎭

Finish backing diag. to centre.

Advanced Technique of the above Figure
    (Not required by the beginner)

Amount of turn: Make ⅜ turn to R. between 1 and 2; make ¼ turn to R. between 4 and 5; make ⅛ turn to R. between 5 and 6.

BEGIN HERE

B

Footwork: 1. T.H.   2. T.   3. T.H.   4. H.T.   5. T.   6. T.H.
Contrary body movement: Used on 1 and 4.
Body sway: Sway to L. on 2 and 3; sway to R. on 5 and 6.

Right Closed Change

LADY

		Music timing	
Begin backing diag. to centre.			
7. Back L.F.	⎫	1	⎫
8. Side R.F.	⎬ No turn.	2	⎬ 1 bar
9. Close L.F. to R.F.	⎭	3	⎭
Finish backing diag. to centre.			

Advanced Technique of the above Figure

(Not required by the beginner)

Amount of turn: Nil.
Footwork: 1. T.H.   2. T.   3. T.H.
Contrary body movement: Used on 1 (slightly).
Body sway: Sway to L. on 2 and 3.

Reverse Turn (Left Turn)

GENTLEMAN

		Music timing	
Begin facing diag. to centre.			
1. Forward L.F.	⎫ Turning to L.	1	⎫
2. Side R.F.	⎬ to	2	⎬ 1 bar
3. Close L.F. to R.F.	⎭ back L.O.D.	3	⎭
4. Back R.F.		1	⎫
5. Side L.F.		2	⎬ 1 bar
6. Close R.F. to L.F.		3	⎭
Finish facing diag. to wall.			

BEGIN
HERE

This fig. may be preceded by:
(1) The Right Closed Change.
(2) The Natural Spin Turn and 4, 5, 6 of the Reverse Turn danced on the side of the ballroom.

This fig. may be followed by:
(1) The Left Closed Change.
(2) 1, 2 and 3 of the Reverse Turn may be followed by the Reverse Corté.

Advanced Technique of the above Figure

(Not required by the beginner)

Amount of turn: Make ¼ turn to L. between 1 and 2; make ⅛ turn to L. between 2 and 3; make ⅜ turn to L. between 4 and 5.
Footwork: 1. H.T.   2. T.   3. T.H.   4. T.H.   5. T.   6. T.H.
Contrary body movement: Used on 1 and 4.
Body sway: Sway to L. on 2 and 3; sway to R. on 5 and 6.

Left Closed Change

GENTLEMAN

Music timing

Begin facing diag. to wall.

7. Forward L.F.
8. Side R.F.   } No turn.
9. Close L.F. to R.F.

1
2   } 1 bar
3

Finish facing diag. to wall.

Advanced Technique of the above Figure

(Not required by the beginner)

Amount of turn: Nil.
Footwork: 1. H.T.   2. T.   3. T.H.
Contrary body movement: Used on 1 (slightly).
Body sway: Sway to L. on 2 and 3.

This fig. may be preceded by:
(1) The Reverse Turn.
(2) The Natural Spin Turn and 4, 5 and 6 of the Reverse Turn (after the Spin).

This fig. may be followed by:
(1) The Natural Turn.
(2) The Natural Spin Turn.

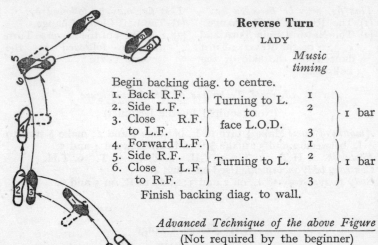

BEGIN HERE

Reverse Turn

LADY

*Music
timing*

Begin backing diag. to centre.

1. Back R.F.	Turning to L.	1
2. Side L.F.	to	2
3. Close R.F. to L.F.	face L.O.D.	3

1 bar

4. Forward L.F.		1
5. Side R.F.	Turning to L.	2
6. Close L.F. to R.F.		3

1 bar

Finish backing diag. to wall.

Advanced Technique of the above Figure

(Not required by the beginner)

Amount of turn: Make ⅜ turn to L. between 1 and 2; make ¼ turn to L. between 4 and 5; make ⅛ turn to L. between 5 and 6.

Footwork: 1. T.H. 2. T. 3. T.H. 4. H.T. 5. T. 6. T.H.
Contrary body movement: Used on 1 and 4.
Body sway: Sway to R. on 2 and 3; sway to L. on 5 and 6.

Left Closed Change

LADY

*Music
timing*

Begin backing diag. to wall.

7. Back R.F.		1
8. Side L.F.	No turn.	2
9. Close R.F. to L.F.		3

1 bar

Finish backing diag. to wall.

Advanced Technique of the above Figure

(Not required by the beginner)

Amount of turn: Nil.
Footwork: 1. T.H. 2. T. 3. T.H.
Contrary body movement: Used on 1 (slightly).
Body sway: Sway to R. on 2 and 3.

Natural Spin Turn

GENTLEMAN

At a corner or along the line of dance.

Music timing

Begin facing diag. to wall.

1. Forward R.F.	⎫ Turning to R. to back	1 ⎫
2. Side L.F.	⎬ L.O.D.	2 ⎬ 1 bar
3. Close R.F. to L.F.	⎭	3 ⎭
4. Back L.F.	⎫ Turning to R. to face original	1 ⎫
5. Forward R.F.	⎬ facing position.	2 ⎬ 1 bar
6. Side L.F.	⎭	3 ⎭

Finish in position, having made one complete turn to R.

Advanced Technique of the above Figure

(Not required by the beginner)

Amount of turn: Make ⅜ turn to R. between 1 and 3; make ⅜ turn to R. on 4; make ¼ turn to R. between 5 and 6.

Footwork: 1. H.T. 2. T. 3. T.H. 4. T.H.T. 5. H.T. 6. T.H.

Contrary body movement: Used on 1, 4 and 5.

Body sway: Sway to R. on 2 and 3.

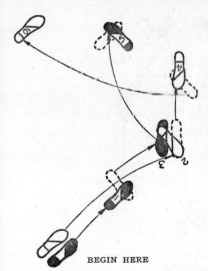

BEGIN HERE

This fig. may be preceded by:
(1) The Left Closed Change.
(2) The Reverse Corté.

This fig. may be followed by:
(1) 4, 5 and 6 of the Reverse Turn;

(a) when the Spin is danced at a corner, dance 4, 5 and 6 of the Reverse Turn with ¼ turn to L., ending diag. to *new wall*;
(b) when Spin is danced on the sides of the ballroom, dance 4, 5 and 6 of the Reverse Turn with ¼ turn to L. to end diag. to centre.
(2) The Reverse Corté, making ¼ turn to L., on 1, 2 and 3 of the Reverse Corté.

Natural Spin Turn

LADY

At a corner or along the line of dance.

Music timing

Begin backing diag. to wall.

1. Back L.F.	} Turning to R. to face	1	}
2. Side R.F.	L.O.D.	2	} 1 bar
3. Close L.F. to R.F.		3	}
4. Forward R.F.	} Turning to	1	}
5. Back L.F.	R. to back	2	} 1 bar
6. Brush R.F. towards L.F. and place it diag. forward.	original position.	3	}

Finish in position having made one complete turn to R.

Advanced Technique of the above Figure

(Not required by the beginner)

Amount of turn: Make ⅜ turn to R. between 1 and 2; make ⅜ turn to R. on 4; make ¼ turn to R. between 5 and 6.

Footwork: 1. T.H. 2. T. 3. T.H. 4. H.T. 5. T. 6. T.H.

Contrary body movement: Used on 1 and 4.

Body sway: Sway to L. on 2 and 3.

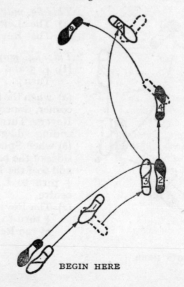

BEGIN HERE

Reverse Corté

GENTLEMAN

Begin backing L.O.D., having danced 1, 2 and 3 of the Reverse Turn.

			Music timing	
1.	Back R.F.		1	
2.	Close L.F. to R.F.	Turning to	2	
3.	Hesitate, holding position with weight on R.F.	L. to face diag to wall.	3	1 bar
4.	Back L.F., P.O.		1	
5.	Side R.F. (in front of partner).	No turn.	2	1 bar
6.	Close L.F. to R.F.		3	

Finish facing diag. to wall.

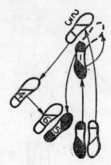

BEGIN HERE

This fig. may be preceded by:
(1) 1, 2 and 3 of the Reverse Turn.
(2) The Natural Spin Turn at a corner.
(3) The Natural Spin Turn on the sides of the ballroom, when the Corté will end facing diag. to centre.

This fig. may be followed by:
(1) The Natural Turn.
(2) The Natural Spin Turn.
(3) The Right Closed Change when the Corté has been danced following the Natural Spin Turn danced on the side of the ballroom.

Advanced Technique of the above Figure

(Not required by the beginner)

Amount of turn: Make ⅜ turn to L. between 1 and 2.
Footwork: 1. T.H. 2. H. of L.F., then T. of both F. 3. T.H. of R.F. 4. T.H. 5. T. 6. T.H.
Contrary body movement: Used on 1 and 4.
Body sway: Sway to R. on 2 and 3; sway to L. on 5 and 6.

Reverse Corté

LADY

Music timing

Begin facing L.O.D., having danced 1, 2, 3 of the Reverse Turn.

1. Forward L.F.	Turning to	1
2. Side R.F.	L. to back	2
3. Close L.F. to R.F.	diag. to wall.	3
4. Forward R.F., O.P.		1
5. Side L.F. (partner in in front).	No turn.	2
6. Close R.F. to L.F.		3

1. Forward L.F. ⎫ Turning to ⎪ 1 ⎫
2. Side R.F. ⎬ L. to back ⎪ 2 ⎬ 1 bar
3. Close L.F. to R.F. ⎭ diag. to wall. ⎪ 3 ⎭
4. Forward R.F., O.P. ⎫ ⎪ 1 ⎫
5. Side L.F. (partner in in front). ⎬ No turn. ⎪ 2 ⎬ 1 bar
6. Close R.F. to L.F. ⎭ ⎪ 3 ⎭

Finish backing diag. to wall.

BEGIN HERE

Advanced Technique of the above Figure

(Not required by the beginner)

Amount of turn: Make ¼ turn to L. between 1 and 2; make ⅛ turn to L. between 2 and 3.

Footwork: 1. H.T. 2. T. 3. T.H. 4. H.T. 5. T. 6. T.H.

Contrary body movement: Used on 1 and 4.

Body sway: Sway to L. on 2 and 3; sway to R. on 5 and 6.

PART II

FOR THOSE WHO ARE NO LONGER BEGINNERS

CHAPTER V

MORE ADVANCED TECHNIQUE

PART I of this book was addressed primarily to beginners
in ballroom dancing. The basic technique and the figures
it described are all that are necessary for the beginner to
take the floor with confidence and enjoyment after a minimum of
practice. But as his experience of the ballroom grows, the novice
will naturally become ambitious to broaden his horizon. In the
Waltz, for instance, he will see other dancers performing figures
which are new to him, and the individual charms of the Foxtrot,
Quickstep, Samba, Rumba, Tango and Viennese Waltz, will
quickly make their appeal.

It is at this stage of the less-experienced dancer's progress that
Part II of this book becomes important. It deals with each of the
dances in turn and introduces new aspects of technique—such as
footwork, body sway and contrary body movement—with which
the beginner has so far not had to concern himself. Study and
practice of the pages which follow will, I am quite sure, bring
their reward in the increased enjoyment that waits on accom-
plishment.

How to Construct The Dances

When you have mastered a few figures in a dance, it is necessary to consider the best way to join them one to the other.

The correct combinations or sequences are more a matter of
practice and experience than anything else, but below the
gentleman's description of each figure I have given the best
figures to use after doing the figure described.

You should aim to get a continuous flowing dance without
unnecessary breaks to spoil the continuity of movement.

According to your ability and experience, you can add other
figures, but it is much better to make sure of a few basic figures
and how to amalgamate them before attempting anything more
advanced.

Footwork

Footwork refers to the rise and fall in the feet, indicating which part of the foot is in contact with the floor on each step or part of a step.

The terms used to describe footwork are:

H. = Heel. (*Note*. This term when used on its own means "Heel onto flat foot", as in a forward walk.)
T. = Toe.
B. = Ball of foot.
Inside edge of foot.
Inside edge of T. (toe).
Inside edge of B. (ball).
Whole foot.
Example:

The Quarter Turns

Footwork	Meaning of footwork
1. H.T.	Heel rising to toe.
2. T.	Toe.
3. T.	Toe.
4. T.H.	Toe lowering to heel.
5. T.H.	Toe lowering to heel.
6. H.	Heel.
7. H. (R.F.) pressure on T. of L.F.	Heel of right foot with pressure on toe of left foot.
8. H.	Heel (then flat).

Contrary Body Movement

For any dancer who wishes to attain the highest standard, it is necessary to have a thorough knowledge, both in theory and practice, of what is known as contrary body movement.

To teach this to a beginner is futile: it cannot be learnt in a few lessons, and it is ridiculous to attempt it. It is reserved solely for those who have acquired good balance and movement. For a professional it is an essential of the utmost importance.

To put it briefly, contrary body movement makes the difference between a straight line and a curve. In ballroom dancing these curves are obtained by turning your body slightly so that the opposite hip and shoulder are towards the leg that you are stepping with.

The four ways that contrary body movement can be used are as follows:

Step forward with the R.F., turning the L. hip and shoulder forward.

Step forward with the L.F., turning the R. hip and shoulder forward.

Step back with the R.F., turning the L. hip and shoulder backward.

Step back with the L.F., turning the R. hip and shoulder backward.

Contrary movement must not be used indiscriminately: it is only used at certain times and in certain places, and I have mentioned where it should be used under my descriptions of the different figures. It is used at the commencement of practically every turning movement to assist you to turn.

It is important to remember that the opposite hip and shoulder should turn as you take your step, not after you have taken it.

Another very important point to remember when using contrary body movement is that it must be used by the entire body from the hips upwards. The commonest fault is for a person to break at the waist, turning the shoulders only. The entire trunk of the body must always turn in one piece without any break in the middle—at the waist.

Another useful hint is to allow your back foot to turn inwards very slightly when using contrary body movement. Actually it is only pointing the way that you are facing, but if you *think* of it as being turned inwards slightly, it will help you a lot. The tendency with most people is to turn the back foot outwards. Doing this pulls on the hip muscles and prevents the hips from turning with the shoulders.

There is another form of contrary body movement, known as contrary body movement position, which occurs when taking a step across your body. If you take a step forward with your right foot across to your left, keeping your body facing front, it will be noticed that you get the same effect as if you stepped straight forward with your right foot, at the same time turning your left hip and shoulder forward.

This second form of contrary movement—contrary body movement position—is used on all "outside" steps; that is, on any variation where you step outside your partner or your partner steps outside you. It is also much used in the Tango, and it occurs sometimes in other figures in ballroom dancing.

The border line between contrary body movement and contrary body movement position is so slight that it is sometimes difficult to differentiate between the two.

Body Sway

A slight sway of the body is introduced into the majority of turning figures in ballroom dancing in order to help to retain good balance, and the inclination of the body should always be towards the centre of the turn that is being made. It also occurs in certain other figures apart from turns.

In a ballroom you always dance anti-clockwise and there are only two basic ways that you can turn—natural (right-handed) or reverse (left-handed). You will appreciate, therefore, that in a Natural Turn you always sway slightly towards the middle of the ballroom, and in a Reverse Turn you always sway slightly towards the outside of the ballroom—the wall.

Another and perhaps easier way of thinking of this is as follows:

For the Quickstep and Slow Foxtrot

If you have taken a "slow" step forward or backward with your right foot, then you sway to the right on the two "quick" steps following.

If you have taken a "slow" step forward or backward with your left foot, then you sway to the left on the two "quick" steps following.

There are exceptions, but as a general rule the above applies.

For the Waltz

If you have taken the 1 forward or backward with your right foot, then you sway to the right for the 2 and 3.

If you have taken the 1 forward or backward with your left foot, then you sway to the left for the 2 and 3.

There are exceptions, but as a general rule the above applies.

The sway when introduced in these dances should be carried from the feet upwards, so that the whole of your body—legs, hips, shoulders and head—is inclined towards the centre of the turn that you are making. If a straight line were drawn through your body as this slight sway was introduced, it should divide you equally into two parts so that no one part should overlap.

Do not forget that the sway must be very slight. Should you have any doubt whatsoever as to which way you should incline, leave it out altogether until you can get a professional to explain it to you.

Remember in no circumstances to attempt this unless you have mastered good balance and can construct your dances without any difficulty.

In the Tango, in basic figures there is no body sway at all.

TABLE GIVING TIMES, TEMPI AND RHYTHMS

NOTE.—As many dance bands play at varying tempi, I am giving in this table the ideal tempo for each dance, and in parenthesis the minimum and maximum tempi that it is possible to dance to. The ideal tempo allows for natural length strides.

Dance	Time	Tempo	No. of Basic Rhythms Used
Quickstep	4/4	48 bars per min. (38 to 54)	Two. 1. Slow. 2. Quick, quick, slow (chassé). (Slows take 2 beats of the music. Quicks take 1 beat of the music.)
Waltz	3/4	30 bars per min. (28 to 34)	One. A step to each beat except when hesitation steps are introduced.
Slow Foxtrot	4/4	30 bars per min. (28 to 36)	Two. 1. Slow. 2. Quick, quick, slow. (Slows take 2 beats. Quicks take 1 beat.)
Tango	2/4	32 bars per min. (28 to 34)	Two. 1. Slow (walk). 2. Quick, quick, slow. (Slows take 1 beat. Quicks take $\frac{1}{2}$ beat.)
Rumba	4/4	40 bars per min. (36 to 48)	One. Slow, slow, quick. (Slows take $\frac{3}{8}$ bar. Quicks take $\frac{1}{4}$ bar.)
Samba	2/4	58 bars per min. (45 to 65)	Four. 1. Slow, slow. 2. Slow, quick, quick. 3. Slow *and* slow. (The value of the first slow is $\frac{3}{4}$ beat, the "and" $\frac{1}{4}$ beat, the final slow 1 beat.) 4. Quick, quick, quick, quick. (Slows take 1 beat. Quicks take $\frac{1}{2}$ beat.)
Viennese Waltz	3/4	56 bars per min. (44 to 60)	One. A step to each beat of the music.

METRONOME BEATS FOR THE MODERN DANCES

Quickstep	96 minim beats per minute.
Waltz	90 crotchet ,, ,, ,,
Slow Foxtrot	120 crotchet ,, ,, ,,
Tango	128 quaver ,, ,, ,,
Rumba	80 minim ,, ,, ,,
Samba	116 crotchet ,, ,, ,,
Viennese Waltz	168 crotchet ,, ,, ,,

Chapter VI

THE WALTZ

THE fundamentals of the Waltz were described in Part I of this book. The pages which follow give details of a number of additional Waltz figures and the standard variations.

Hesitation Change

This figure is very useful in small or rather crowded ballrooms; it will change you quickly from the Natural into the Reverse Turn, but it needs very careful leading and therefore is not suitable for the complete beginner.

GENTLEMAN

Begin facing diag. to wall and finish facing diag. to centre.
1, 2, 3, 4. Do 1, 2, 3, 4 of the Natural Turn, then:

Heel Pull { 5. Pull R.F. back to side of L.F., turning from L. heel on to R.F. (feet slightly apart).
6. Hesitate, brushing L.F. to R.F. (weight on R.F.).

Amount of turn: Make ⅜ turn to R. between 1 and 3; make ⅜ turn to R. between 4 and 5.
Footwork: 1. H.T. 2. T. 3. T.H. 4. T.H. 5. H., inside edge of foot, whole foot. 6. Inside edge of T. (L.F.).
Contrary body movement: Used on 1 and 4.
Body sway: 1, 2, 3, as in the Natural Turn. Sway to L. on 5 and 6.

LADY

Begin backing diag. to wall and finish backing diag. to centre.
1, 2, 3, 4. Do 1, 2, 3, 4 of the Natural Turn, then:
5. Side L.F.
6. Hesitate, brushing R.F. to L.F. (weight on L.F.).
Amount of turn: Make ⅜ turn to R. between 1 and 2; make ⅜ turn to R. between 4 and 5.
Footwork: 1. T.H. 2. T. 3. T.H. 4. H.T. 5. T.H. 6. Inside edge of T. (R.F.).
Contrary body movement: Used on 1 and 4.
Body sway: 1, 2, 3, as in the Natural Turn. Sway to R. on 5 and 6.

This fig. may be preceded by:
(1) The Left Closed Change.
(2) The Reverse Corté.
(3) The Telemark.
(4) The Outside Spin.
(5) The Open Telemark.
(6) Steps 4, 5 and 6 can be danced after the Passing Change Reverse to the Natural, Drag Hesitation, or Backward Lock.

This fig. may be followed by:
(1) The Reverse Turn.
(2) The Double Reverse Spin.
(3) 1, 2 and 3 of the Reverse Turn to Passing Change.
(4) The Telemark.
(5) The Open Telemark.
(6) The Drag Hesitation.

Passing Change (Natural to Reverse)

GENTLEMAN

Begin backing diag. to centre and finish backing L.O.D.
1. Back L.F.
2. Back R.F., curving towards L.O.D.
3. Back L.F.

Amount of turn: Make ⅛ turn to R. between 1 and 3.
Footwork: 1. T.H. 2. T. 3. T.H.
Contrary body movement: Used on 1.
Body sway: Sway to L. on 2 and 3.

LADY

Begin facing diag. to centre and finish facing L.O.D.
1. Forward R.F.
2. Forward L.F., curving towards L.O.D.
3. Forward R.F.

Amount of turn: Make ⅛ turn to R. between 1 and 3.
Footwork: 1. H.T. 2. T. 3. T.H.
Contrary body movement: Used on 1.
Body sway: Sway to R. on 2 and 3.

This fig. may be preceded by:
(1) 1, 2 and 3 of the Natural Right Turn (ended backing diag. to centre).

This fig. may be followed by:
(1) 4, 5 and 6 of the Reverse Left Turn.
(2) The Reverse Corté.

Passing Change (Reverse to Natural)

GENTLEMAN

Begin backing diag. to wall and finish backing L.O.D.
1. Back R.F.
2. Back L.F., curving towards L.O.D.
3. Back R.F.
Amount of turn: Make ⅛ turn to L. between 1 and 3.
Footwork: 1. T.H. 2. T. 3. T.H.
Contrary body movement: Used on 1.
Body sway: Sway to R. on 2 and 3.

LADY

Begin facing diag. to wall and finish facing L.O.D.
1. Forward L.F.
2. Forward R.F., curving towards L.O.D.
3. Forward L.F.
Amount of turn: Make ⅛ turn to L. between 1 and 3.
Footwork: 1. H.T. 2. T. 3. T.H.
Contrary body movement: Used on 1.
Body sway: Sway to L. on 2 and 3.

This fig. may be preceded by:
(1) 1, 2 and 3 of the Reverse Left Turn (ended backing diag. to wall).

This fig. may be followed by:
(1) 4, 5 and 6 of the Natural Right Turn.
(2) 4, 5 and 6 of the Hesitation Change.
(3) 4, 5 and 6 of the Natural Spin Turn.
(4) The Impetus Turn or the Open Impetus Turn.

The Whisk

GENTLEMAN

Begin and finish facing diag. to wall.
1. Forward L.F.
2. Side R.F., slightly forward.
3. Cross L.F. behind R.F. in P.P.
Amount of turn: Nil.
Footwork: 1. H.T. 2. T. 3. T.H.
Contrary body movement: Used on 1.
Body sway: Sway to L. on 2 and 3.

The Whisk

LADY

Begin backing diag. to wall and finish facing diag. to centre.
1. Back R.F.
2. Diag. back L.F.
3. Cross R.F. behind L.F. in P.P.
Amount of turn: Make ¼ turn to R. between 1 and 2.
Footwork: 1. T.H.   2. T.   3. T.H.
Contrary body movement: Nil.
Body sway: Sway to R. on 2 and 3.

This fig. may be preceded by:
(1) The Reverse Left Turn.
(2) The Double Reverse Spin (ended facing diag. to wall).

This fig. may be followed by:
(1) The Syncopated Chassé.
(2) The Wing.

Syncopated Chassé

This figure is preceded by the Whisk.

GENTLEMAN

Begin and finish facing diag. to wall.
1. Step through with R.F. in P.P.
2. Side L.F. slightly forward.
   "and". Close R.F. to L.F., turning partner to face you.
3. Side L.F., preparing to step outside partner.
This figure is followed by a step forward, R.F. outside partner, into any Natural figure.
Amount of turn: Nil.
Footwork: 1. H.T.   2. T., "and", T.   3. T.H.
Contrary body movement: Used on 1.
Body sway: Nil.

LADY

Begin facing diag. to centre and finish backing diag. to wall.
1. Step through with L.F. in P.P.
2. Side R.F. slightly back.
   "and". Close L.F. to R.F., turning to face partner.
3. Side R.F.
This figure is followed by a step back, L.F., partner outside, into a Natural figure.
Amount of turn: Make ¼ turn to L. between 1, 2 and "and".
Footwork: 1. H.T.   2. T.   3. T.   4. T.H.
Contrary body movement: Used on 1.
Body sway: Nil.
Note. Both the gentleman and lady dance four steps to three beats. The second beat is the split beat (not the third). It helps to count s.q.q.s. for this figure instead of 1, 2 "and", 3.

Closed Telemark

The pattern is the same as that used in the Slow Foxtrot but counted 1, 2, 3.

The Closed Telemark is usually preceded by the Wing, or the Double Reverse Spin.

It is followed by any Natural figure.

See page 70.

Impetus Turn

The pattern is the same as that used in the Slow Foxtrot but counted 1, 2, 3.

The Impetus Turn is usually preceded by 1, 2, 3 of the Natural Turn, the Drag Hesitation or the Backward Lock.

It is followed by 4, 5, 6 of the Reverse Turn, or the Reverse Corté. See page 69.

Open Telemark

GENTLEMAN

Begin facing diag. to centre and finish diag. to wall in P.P.

1. Forward L.F. } turning to L. to back diag. to wall.
2. Side R.F.
3. Side L.F., slightly forward in P.P.

Amount of turn: Make ¼ turn to L. between 1 and 2; make ½ turn to L. between 2 and 3.

Footwork: 1. H.T. 2. T. 3. T.H.

Contrary body movement: Used on 1.

Body sway: Sway to L. on 2.

LADY

Begin backing diag. to centre and finish in P.P. with feet pointing to L.O.D.

1. Back R.F., turning to L.
2. Close L.F. to R.F. (heel turn to face L.O.D.).
3. Diag. forward, R.F. in P.P.

Amount of turn: Make ⅜ turn to L. between 1 and 2.

Footwork: 1. T.H. 2. H.T. 3. T.H.

Contrary body movement: Used on 1.

Body sway: Sway to R. on 2.

This fig. may be preceded by:
(1) The Right Closed Change.
(2) The Double Reverse Spin.
(3) The Natural Spin Turn, 4, 5 and 6 of the Reverse Left Turn (ended diag. to centre).
(4) The Wing.

This fig. may be followed by:
(1) The Wing.
(2) The Cross Hesitation.

Cross Hesitation

GENTLEMAN

Begin and finish according to preceding and following figs.

1. Forward R.F., in P.P. and C.B.M.P.
2. Close L.F. to R.F. (weight on R.F.).
3. Hesitate with weight on R.F.

Amount of turn: Nil or $\frac{1}{4}$ turn to L. may be made between 1 and 2.
Footwork: 1. H.T.   2. T. (both feet).   3. T.H. (R.F.)
Contrary body movement: Nil.
Body sway: Nil.

LADY

Begin and finish according to preceding and following figs.

1. Forward L.F., and across in P.P. and C.B.M.P.
2. Side R.F.
3. Close L.F. to R.F.

Amount of turn: Make $\frac{1}{4}$ turn to L. between 1 and 2; make $\frac{1}{8}$ turn to L. between 2 and 3.
Footwork: 1. H.T.   2. T.   3. T.H.
Contrary body movement: Used on 1.
Body sway: Sway to L. on 2 and 3.

This fig. may be preceded by:
(1) The Open Telemark.
(2) The Whisk.
(3) The Open Impetus Turn.

This fig. may be followed by:
(1) L.F. back (lady R.F. forward) into 4, 5 and 6 of Reverse Corté.
(2) The Outside Spin.
(3) L.F. forward (lady R.F. back) into the Left Closed Change or the Whisk.

Notes. (1) No turn on the Cross Hesitation (for gentleman) when used after the Open Telemark or the Whisk.
(2) $\frac{1}{4}$ turn to L. may be made after the Open Impetus Turn has been danced into the Cross Hesitation, when the Cross Hesitation may be followed by the Backward Lock Step.

The Wing

This figure is usually preceded by the Open Telemark, taking the third step slightly further back than normally.

GENTLEMAN

Begin in P.P. after the Open Telemark and finish along L.O.D. or diag. to centre.

1. Forward R.F., and across in P.P. and C.B.M.P. (pointing to L.O.D.)
2, 3. Keeping weight on R.F., close L.F. to R.F.

Amount of turn: Make $\frac{1}{8}$ turn to L. between 3 of the Open Telemark and 1 of the Wing; make $\frac{1}{8}$ turn to L. between 2 and 3.

Footwork: 1. H. 2, 3. Pressure on T. of R.F. with F. flat, and pressure on inside edge of T. of L.F.

Contrary body movement: Nil.

Body sway: Nil.

LADY

Begin in P.P. after the Open Telemark and finish facing against L.O.D. or backing diag. to centre.

1. Forward L.F., in P.P. and C.B.M.P.
2. Forward R.F., preparing to step O.P. on his L. side.
3. Forward L.F., in C.B.M.P., O.P. on his L. side.

Amount of turn: Make $\frac{1}{8}$ turn to L. between 3 of the Open Telemark and 1 of the Wing; make $\frac{3}{8}$ turn to L. between 1 and 3 of the Wing.

Footwork: 1. H.T. 2. T. 3. T.H.

Contrary body movement: Used on 1.

Body sway: Sway to L. on 2 and 3.

This fig. may be preceded by:
(1) The Open Telemark.
(2) The Whisk.

This fig. may be followed by:
(1) The Reverse Turn, taking first step O.P. (gentleman).
(2) The Double Reverse Spin, taking first step O.P.
(3) The Telemark, taking first step O.P.
(4) The Drag Hesitation, taking first step O.P.

Open Impetus Turn

This figure is preceded by 1, 2 and 3 of the Natural Turn.

GENTLEMAN

Begin backing L.O.D. and finish diag. to centre in P.P.
1. Back L.F., turning to R.
2. Close R.F. to L.F., turning from L. heel on to R.F. (heel turn) to face diag. to centre.
3. Diag. forward L.F. in P.P.

Amount of turn: Make ⅜ turn to R. between 1 and 2.
Footwork: 1. T.H.   2. H.T.   3. T.H.
Contrary body movement: Used on 1.
Body sway: Sway to L. on 2.

LADY

Begin facing L.O.D. and finish diag. to centre in P.P.
1. Forward R.F. ⎫
2. Side L.F.   ⎬ Turning to R. to back diag. to centre.
                 ⎭
3. Brush R.F. to L.F. and step to side with R.F. in P.P.

Amount of turn: Make ⅜ turn to R. between 1 and 2; make ⅜ turn to R. between 2 and 3.
Footwork: 1. H.T.   2. T.   3. T.H.
Contrary body movement: Used on 1.
Body sway: Sway to R. on 2.

This fig. may be preceded by:
(1) 1, 2 and 3 of the Natural Turn.
(2) The Drag Hesitation.
(3) The Backward Lock.

This fig. may be followed by:
(1) The Cross Hesitation.
(2) The Wing.
(3) The Right Closed Change, commenced in P.P.

Drag Hesitation

GENTLEMAN

Begin facing L.O.D., or diag. to centre, and finish backing diag. to wall.
1. Forward L.F.
2. Side R.F.
3. Close L.F. to R.F., keeping weight on R.F., preparing to lead P.O. on R. side.

Amount of turn: Make ⅜ or ¼ turn to L. between 1 and 3.
Footwork: 1. H.T.   2. T.   3. T. (of both feet), then T.H. (R.F.).
Contrary body movement: Used on 1.
Body sway: Nil.

Drag Hesitation

LADY

Begin backing L.O.D., or back diag. to centre, and finish facing diag. to wall.

1. Back R.F.
2. Side L.F.
3. Close R.F. to L.F., keeping weight on L.F., preparing to step O.P. on R. side.

Amount of turn: Make ⅜ or ¼ turn to L. between 1 and 3.
Footwork: 1. T.H. 2. T. 3. T. (of both feet), then T.H. (L.F.).
Contrary body movement: Used on 1.
Body sway: Nil.

This fig. may be preceded by:	This fig. may be followed by:
(1) The Hesitation Change.	(1) 4, 5 and 6 of the Natural Turn.
(2) The Right Closed Change.	
(3) The Double Reverse Spin.	(2) The Backward Lock.
(4) The Wing.	(3) The Impetus Turn or the Open Impetus Turn.
(5) 4, 5 and 6 of the Reverse Turn after the Natural Spin Turn.	(4) 4, 5 and 6 of the Hesitation Change.

Backward Lock

GENTLEMAN

Begin and finish backing diag. to wall.

1. Back L.F., in C.B.M.P., P.O.
2. Back R.F.
   "and". Cross L.F. in front of R.F.
3. Diag. back R.F., preparing to lead P.O. on R. side.

Amount of turn: Nil.
Footwork: 1. T.H. 2. T., "and", T. 3. T.H.
Contrary body movement: Used on 1.
Body sway: Nil.

LADY

Begin and finish facing diag. to wall.

1. Forward R.F., O.P., in C.B.M.P.
2. Diag. forward L.F.
   "and". Cross R.F. behind L.F.
3. Diag. forward L.F., preparing to step O.P. on R. side.

Amount of turn: Nil.
Footwork: 1. H.T. 2. T., "and", T. 3. T.H.
Contrary body movement: Used on 1.
Body sway: Nil.

Notes. (1) Both the gentleman and lady dance four steps to three beats. The second beat is the split beat (not the third). It helps to count s.Q.Q.s. for this figure instead of 1, 2 "and", 3.

(2) While the gentleman dances the Backward Lock backwards, the lady dances her steps forwards.

This fig. may be preceded by:
(1) The Drag Hesitation.

This fig. may be followed by:
(1) 4, 5 and 6 of the Natural Turn.
(2) The Impetus Turn or the Open Impetus Turn.

Double Reverse Spin

Although called the *Double* Reverse Spin, this does not signify that it must be used twice. More often than not, it is only used once at a time.

Whilst the gentleman does three steps to three beats, the lady does four steps to three beats, that is why it is counted 1, 2 "and", 3.

GENTLEMAN

Begin and finish according to preceding and following figs.

1. Forward L.F. ⎫
2. Side R.F. ⎬ Turning to L. to back diag. to wall.

Toe ⎰ "and". Close L.F. towards R.F., turning on R.F.
Pivot ⎱ 3. Complete turn on R.F. (retaining weight on R.F.).

Amount of turn: Make complete turn or ¾ turn to L., according to the preceding and following figs.

Notes. (1) When a complete turn is made: make ⅜ turn to L. between 1 and 2, and make ⅝ turn to L. between 2 and 3.

(2) When ¾ turn is to be made: make ⅜ turn to L. between 1 and 2, and make ⅜ turn to L. between 2 and 3.

Footwork: 1. H.T. 2. T. "and", 3. T. of L.F., then T.H. of R.F.
Contrary body movement: Used on 1.
Body sway: Nil.

LADY

Begin and finish according to preceding and following figs.

1. R.F. back. ⎫
2. Close L.F. to R.F. (heel turn) ⎬ Turning to L. to face L.O.D.
"and". Side R.F. slightly back. ⎭
3. Cross L.F. in front of R.F.

Amount of turn: Make complete turn to L. or ¾ turn, according to the preceding and following figs.

Notes. (1) When a complete turn is made: make ½ turn to L. between 1 and 2; make ⅜ turn between 2 and "and"; and make ⅛ between "and" and 3.

(2) When ¾ turn is made: make ⅜ turn to L. between 1 and 2; make ¼ turn between 2 and "and"; and make ⅛ turn between "and" and 3.

Footwork: 1. T.H. 2. H.T., "and", T. 3. T.H.
Contrary body movement: Used on 1.
Body sway: Nil.

This fig. may be preceded by:	*This fig. may be followed by:*
(1) The Right Closed Change.	(1) The Left Closed Change.
(2) The Hesitation Change.	(2) 1, 2 and 3 of the Reverse Turn
(3) The Natural Spin Turn and 4,	into the Passing Change.
5 and 6 of the Reverse Turn.	(3) The Double Reverse Spin.
(4) The Reverse Turn.	(4) The Telemark.
(5) The Double Reverse Spin.	(5) The Open Telemark.
(6) The Wing.	(6) The Drag Hesitation.
	(7) The Whisk.

Outside Spin

GENTLEMAN

Begin and finish facing diag. to wall.
1. Very short step back L.F., pivoting on it to R., in C.B.M.P.
2. Forward R.F., O.P., in C.B.M.P.
3. Side L.F., still turning, to end with L.F. back.
Amount of turn: Make $\frac{3}{8}$ turn to R. on 1; make $\frac{3}{8}$ turn to R. between
   2 and 3; make $\frac{1}{4}$ turn to R. on 3.
Footwork: 1. T.H.T. 2. H.T. 3. T.H.
Contrary body movement: Used on 1 and 2.
Body sway: Nil.

LADY

Begin and finish backing diag. to wall.
1. Forward R.F., O.P., in C.B.M.P.
2. Close L.F. to R.F., turning to face wall.
3. Forward R.F. in front of partner, ending in C.B.M.P.
Amount of turn: Make $\frac{3}{8}$ turn to R. between 1 and 2; make $\frac{1}{4}$ turn to
   R. between 2 and 3; make $\frac{1}{4}$ turn to R. on 3.
Contrary body movement: Used on 1.
Body sway: Nil.

This fig. may be preceded by:	*This fig. may be followed by:*
(1) 1, 2 and 3 of the Reverse	(1) Any Natural Fig.
Corté.	
(2) The Open Telemark and the	
Cross Hesitation.	
(3) The Open Impetus Turn and	
the Cross Hesitation.	

CHAPTER VII

THE SLOW FOXTROT

SOME GENERAL NOTES

THE greater part of the technique of modern ballroom dancing has been formed out of this dance, and to anyone who is a serious dancer or intends to take up dancing professionally, a thorough knowledge of the Slow Foxtrot is essential.

For the dancer who cannot give very much time to it, I would advise leaving this dance and beginning with Slow Rhythm, the social dancer's Slow Foxtrot.

The Slow Foxtrot is essentially a good dancer's dance, and its greatest handicap is that it requires a lot of room to dance in comfort. It is very popular at dance halls throughout the country, owing to their spaciousness, but is rarely seen in the smarter ballrooms of London, as these are invariably small and crowded. Slow Rhythm is therefore more suitable for the novice and for crowded or small ballrooms.

The fundamental movements of this dance are the walk and the Three Step, all the basic figures are built up from these two movements.

The walk forward consists of long gliding steps forward taken from the hips, skimming the feet lightly along the floor the whole time.

Start with the feet together. Place the weight of the body on the stationary foot, and with the opposite foot take a long gliding step forward, straight from the hip, with the ball of the foot skimming the floor, going on to the heel as the heel of the foot passes the toes of the stationary foot. The heel of the back foot should now be released gradually from the floor, the moving foot continuing forward on the heel to the full extent of the stride. The weight of the body is now central between the two feet— on the heel of the front foot and the ball of the back foot. The toes of the front foot are then immediately lowered on to the floor and the weight of the body is taken forward over the front foot. The back foot is then brought forward, moving from the toes on to the ball of the foot, until it reaches the front foot, from where the forward movement is repeated as described above.

The walk backward. Swing the leg well back from the hip, going from the ball of the foot out on to the toes. The weight is on the front foot. Release the toes of the front foot (keeping the back heel up). The weight is now central between the two feet (on the heel of the front foot and the ball of the back foot). Pull the front foot back with light pressure on the heel, controlling the weight on the ball of the back foot so that the back heel does not lower until the front foot (which is now flat) passes underneath you. Repeat *ad lib.* with alternate feet. Each walking step takes two beats of the music and is counted "slow."

Note. Walking steps are never used on their own, but all forward slow steps are based on the movement of the walk forward, and all slow steps backwards are based on the movement of the walk backward.

To develop good balance, movement and timing, practise walks forward and backward before attempting the figures.

The Hold is the same as described on page 20.

BEGIN HERE

Feather Step

GENTLEMAN

Begin and finish either facing L.O.D., or diag. to wall, or diag. to centre.

1. Forward R.F.   S.
2. Forward L.F., preparing to step O.P.   Q.
3. Forward R.F., O.P., in C.B.M.P.   Q.
4. Forward L.F. (in front of partner).   S.

Amount of turn: This figure may curve very slightly to R.

Footwork: 1. H.T.   2. T.   3. T.H.   4. H.

Contrary body movement: Used on 1 and 4.

Body sway: Sway to R. on 2 and 3.

Feather Step

LADY

Begin and finish either backing L.O.D., or diag. to
wall, or diag. to centre.

1. Back L.F.   s.
2. Back R.F.   Q.
3. Back L.F., in C.B.M.P., P.O.   Q.
4. Back R.F. (partner in front).   s.

Amount of turn: The lady curves her step slightly
    towards the wall.
Footwork: 1. T.H.   2. T.H.   3. T.H.   4. T.
Contrary body movement: Used on 1 and 4.
Body sway: Sway to L. on 2 and 3.

BEGIN HERE

This fig. may be preceded by:
(1) The Natural Turn.
(2) The Reverse Wave.
(3) The Change of Direction.
(4) The Telemark (first step out-
    side partner).
(5) The Open Telemark (first
    step in P.P.).
(6) The Box (first step outside
    partner).
(7) The Open Impetus (first step
    in P.P.).
(8) The Hover Telemark (first
    step outside partner).
(9) The Outside Swivel (first step
    in P.P.).

This fig. may be followed by:
(1) The Three-Step.
(2) The Reverse Wave (when
    Feather Step is danced diag.
    to wall or along L.O.D.).
(3) The Change of Direction.
(4) The Reverse Turn (when
    Feather Step is danced diag.
    to centre).
(5) The Telemark (when Feather
    Step is danced diag. to centre).
(6) The Hover Telemark (when
    Feather Step is danced diag.
    to wall).
(7) The Box, after any Feather
    Step.
(8) The Open Telemark (when
    Feather Step is danced diag.
    to centre).

Three Step

Begin and finish either facing L.O.D., or facing diag. to wall, or facing diag. to wall and curve to L. to L.O.D.

1. Forward R.F.   Q.
2. Forward L.F.   Q.
3. Forward R.F.   S.

Amount of turn: Nil.; or if curved make about ⅛ turn to L. between 1 and 3.
Footwork: 1. H.T. 2. T.H. 3. H. (*Note.* When step 3 becomes first step of a Natural fig., footwork on 3 will be H.T.).
Contrary body movement: Used on 3.
Body sway: Sway to L. on 1 and 2.
Note. When the Three Step is joined to any Natural fig., the last step of the Three Step becomes the first step of the Natural fig.

Begin and finish either backing L.O.D., or backing diag. to wall, or backing diag. to wall and curve to L. to L.O.D.

1. Back L.F.   Q.
2. Back R.F.   Q.
3. Back L.F.   S.

Amount of turn: Nil; or if curved make about ⅛ turn to L. between 1 and 3.
Footwork: 1. T.H. 2. T.H. 3. T. (*Note.* When step 3 becomes first step of a Natural fig., footwork on 3 will be T.H.)
Contrary body movement: Used on 3.
Body sway: Sway to R. on 1 and 2.
Note. When the Three Step is joined to any Natural fig., the last step of the Three Step becomes the first of the Natural fig.

This fig. may be preceded by:
(1) The Feather Step.
(2) The Reverse Turn or any Feather Finish.
(3) The Hover Feather.
(4) The Natural Hover Telemark.
(5) The Natural Telemark.
(6) The Natural Twist Turn.
(7) The Weave
(8) The Top Spin.

This fig. may be followed by:
(1) Any Natural Turn (i.e. the Natural Hover Telemark, the Natural Twist Turn, etc.).

Natural Turn

GENTLEMAN

Begin facing either L.O.D., or diag. to wall, and finish facing diag
to centre.

> *Note.* The third step of the Three Step becomes the first of
> the Natural Turn.

1. Forward R.F.	s.
2. Side L.F. Turning to R. to back	Q.
3. Back R.F. L.O.D.	Q.
4. Back L.F.	s.

Heel Pull   5. Pull R.F. back to side of L.F., turning
from L. heel on to R.F. (feet slightly
apart), then brush L.F. towards R.F.   s.

6. Forward L.F.   s.

Amount of turn: Make ⅜ or ½ turn to R. between 1
and 3; make ⅜ turn to R. between 4 and 5.

Footwork: 1. H.T.   2. T.   3. T.H.   4. T.H.   5. H.
Inside edge of foot, whole foot, then inside edge of
L.F.   6. H.

Contrary body movement: Used on 1, 4 and 6.

Body sway: Sway to R. on 2 and 3; sway to L. on 5.

Note. The Natural Turn can be danced along the sides
of the room, or round a corner, when less turn would
be made.

This fig. may be preceded by:
(1) The Three Step, making last
step the first of the Natural
Turn.
(2) The Telemark, making last
step the first of the Natural
Turn, but outside partner.

BEGIN HERE

This fig. may be followed by:
(1) The Feather Step.
(2) (In a small ballroom.)
Making last step of the
Natural Turn, first step of
any Reverse figure.

(3) The Hover Feather from fifth
step.
(4) The Impetus Turn, the Open
Impetus, or the Outside
Swivel after third step.

Natural Turn

LADY

Begin backing L.O.D., or backing diag. to wall, and finish backing
diag. to centre.

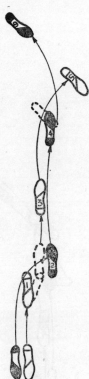

Heel Turn	1. Back L.F. s.

1. Back L.F.   s.

Heel Turn {
2. Close R.F. to L.F. turning from L. heel on to R.F.   } Turning to R. to face L.O.D.   Q.

3. Forward L.F.   Q.
4. Forward R.F., turning to R.   s.
5. Side L.F., then brush R.F. to L.F.   s.
6. Back R.F.   s.

Amount of turn: Make ½ turn to R. between 1 and 2;
make ⅜ turn to R. between 4 and 5.

Footwork: 1. T.H.   2. H.T.   3. T.H.   4. H.T.
5. T.H., then inside edge of T. of R.F.   6. T.

Contrary body movement: Used on 1, 4 and 6.

Body sway: Sway to L. on 2 and 3; sway to R. on 5.

For preceding and following figs. for Natural Turn
see note following description of gentleman's steps.

BEGIN HERE

Reverse Turn

GENTLEMAN

Begin facing diag. to centre and finish facing diag. to wall.

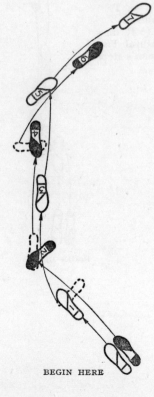

1. Forward L.F.	Turning to L. to back L.O.D.	s.
2. Side R.F.		Q.
3. Back L.F.		Q.
4. Back R.F.		s.
Feather Finish { 5. Side L.F. slightly forward.		Q.
6. Forward R.F., O.P., in C.B.M.P.		Q.
7. Forward L.F. (in front of partner).		s.

Amount of turn: Make ⅜ turn to L. between 1 and 3; make ⅛ turn to L. between 4 and 5.

Footwork: 1. H.T. 2. T. 3. T.H. 4. T.H.T. 5. T. 6. T.H. 7. H.

Contrary body movement: Used on 1, 4 and 7.

Body sway: Sway to L. on 2 and 3; sway to R. on 5 and 6.

Note. The Reverse Turn is danced along the sides of the room only and not used round a corner.

Steps 5, 6 and 7 are similar to 2, 3 and 4 of the Feather Step and are therefore called a Feather Finish.

This fig. may be preceded by:
(1) The Feather Step, danced diag. to centre.
(2) Change of Direction (last step becoming first of Reverse Turn).
(3) The Hover Feather.
(4) The Natural Telemark.
(5) The Natural Hover Telemark.
(6) The Natural Twist Turn.
(7) The Top Spin.

This fig. may be followed by:
(1) The Three Step.
(2) The Reverse Wave.
(3) The Change of Direction.
(4) The Box.
(5) The Hover Telemark.
(6) The Top Spin after sixth step.

BEGIN HERE

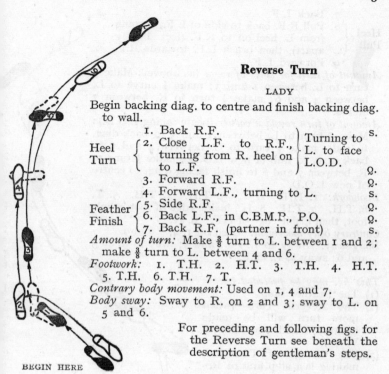

BEGIN HERE

Reverse Turn

LADY

Begin backing diag. to centre and finish backing diag. to wall.

Heel Turn {
1. Back R.F.
2. Close L.F. to R.F., turning from R. heel on to L.F.
} Turning to L. to face L.O.D.
         s.
         Q.

3. Forward R.F.   Q.
4. Forward L.F., turning to L.   s.

Feather Finish {
5. Side R.F.
6. Back L.F., in C.B.M.P., P.O.
7. Back R.F. (partner in front)
}
   Q.
   Q.
   s.

Amount of turn: Make ⅜ turn to L. between 1 and 2; make ⅜ turn to L. between 4 and 6.

Footwork: 1. T.H. 2. H.T. 3. T.H. 4. H.T. 5. T.H. 6. T.H. 7. T.

Contrary body movement: Used on 1, 4 and 7.

Body sway: Sway to R. on 2 and 3; sway to L. on 5 and 6.

For preceding and following figs. for the Reverse Turn see beneath the description of gentleman's steps.

Reverse Wave

GENTLEMAN

Begin facing L.O.D. and finish facing diag. to centre.

1. Forward L.F.
2. Side R.F.
3. Back L.F.
} Turning to L. to back diag. to wall.
   s.
   Q.
   Q.

4. Back R.F.
5. Back L.F.
6. Back R.F.
} curving to L. to back L.O.D.
   s.
   Q.
   Q.

7. Back L.F.   s.

Heel { 8. Pull R.F. back to side of L.F., turning
Pull {   from L. heel on to R.F. (feet slightly
{   apart), then brush L.F. towards R.F.   s.

9. Forward L.F.   s.

Amount of turn for sides of room (as above): Make ⅜
turn to L. between 1 and 3; make ⅛ curve to L.
between 4 and 6; make ⅜ turn to R. between 7
and 8.

Amount of turn round a corner (begin facing L.O.D.):
Make ⅜ turn to L. between 1 and 3 to back diag.
to wall; make ¼ turn to L. between 4 and 6 to
back diag. to wall of new L.O.D.; make ¼ turn to
R. between 7 and 8 to finish facing diag. to centre
of new L.O.D.

Footwork: 1. H.T. 2. T. 3. T.H. 4. T.H. 5. T.
6. T.H. 7. T.H. 8. H., inside edge of foot, whole
foot, then inside edge of L.F. 9. H.

Contrary body movement: Used on 1, 4, 7 and 9.

Body sway: Sway to L. on 2 and 3; sway to R. on 5
and 6; sway to L. on 8.

BEGIN HERE

This fig. may be preceded by:
(1) The Feather Step.
(2) The Reverse Turn (when
more turn will be made
between 1 and 3 of Reverse
Wave).
(3) The Change of Direction,
making last step first of Reverse Wave.
(4) The Hover Feather.
(5) The Natural Telemark.
(6) The Natural Hover Telemark.
(7) The Natural Twist Turn.
(8) The Weave.
(9) The Top Spin.
(10) Any Feather Finish.

This fig. may be followed by:
(1) The Feather Step.
(2) The Impetus Turn after sixth
step of the Wave.
(3) The Hover Feather after
eighth step.
(4) The Weave after fourth step
of the Wave.
(5) The Open Impetus after sixth
step of the Wave.

Reverse Wave

LADY

Begin backing L.O.D. and finish backing diag. to centre.

Heel Turn
{
1. Back R.F., turning to L.
2. Close L.F. to R.F., turning from R. heel on to L.F.
}
Turning to L. to face diag. to wall.
s.
Q.

3. Forward R.F. Q.
4. Forward L.F. S.
5. Forward R.F. } Curving to L. to face Q.
6. Forward L.F. } L.O.D. Q.
7. Forward R.F. S.
8. Side L.F., then brush R.F. to L.F. S.
9. Back R.F. S.

Amount of turn for sides of room (as above): Make ⅜ turn to L. between 1 and 2; make ⅛ curve to L. between 4 and 6; make ⅜ turn to R. between 7 and 8.

Footwork: 1. T.H. 2. H.T. 3. T.H. 4. H. 5. H.T. 6. T.H. 7. H.T. 8. T.H., then inside edge of T. of R.F. 9. T.

Amount of turn round a corner (begin backing L.O.D.): Make ⅜ turn to L. between 1 and 2 to face diag. to wall; make ¼ turn to L. between 4 and 6 to face diag. to wall of new L.O.D.; make ¼ turn to R. between 7 and 8 to finish backing diag. to centre of new L.O.D.

Contrary body movement: Used on 1, 4, 7 and 9.

Body sway: Sway to R. on 2 and 3; sway to L. on 5 and 6; sway to R. on 8.

For preceding and following figs. for the Reverse Wave see beneath the description of gentleman's steps.

BEGIN HERE

Change of Direction

This figure is commenced on the last step of the Feather Step, or on the last step of the Reverse Turn, when at the end of the room, in a corner, or when you have not enough space to follow either of these figures with a Three Step and Natural Turn.

GENTLEMAN

Begin and finish according to the preceding and following figure.

1. Forward L.F.		s.
2. Diagonally forward R.F.	⎫ Turning to L.	Q. ⎫
3. Close L.F. to R.F., slightly forward, without weight (relaxing both knees).	⎬	⎬ or s.
	⎭	Q. ⎭
4. Forward L.F. in C.B.M.P.		s.

Amount of turn: Make up to ½ turn (or less) to L.

Footwork: 1. H. 2 and 3. Inside edge of T., H., then inside edge of T. of L.F. 4. H.

Contrary body movement: Used on 1 and 4.

Body sway: Sway to L. on 2 and 3.

Note. In standard technique, steps 2 and 3 are timed as one "slow".

LADY

Begin and finish according to the preceding and following figure.

1. Back R.F.		s.
2. Diag. back L.F.	⎫ Turning to L.	Q. ⎫
3. Close R.F. to L.F., slightly back, without weight (relaxing both knees).	⎬	⎬ or s.
	⎭	Q. ⎭
4. Back R.F. in C.B.M.P.		s.

Amount of turn: Make up to ½ turn (or less) to L.

Footwork: 1. T.H. 2 and 3. T., inside edge of T., H., then inside edge of T. of R.F. 4. T.

Contrary body movement: Used on 1 and 4.

Body sway: Sway to R. on 2 and 3.

This fig. may be preceded by:
(1) The Feather Step.
(2) The Reverse Turn.
(3) The Hover Feather.
(4) The Natural Twist Turn.
(5) The Natural Hover Telemark.
(6) The Natural Telemark.
(7) The Top Spin.
(8) The Weave.
(9) Any Feather Finish.

This fig. may be followed by:
(1) The Feather Step, or the last step of the Change of Direction may be used as first of a Reverse fig.

Note. After these figures have been mastered, you should have no difficulty in introducing more advanced figures such as the Telemarks and the Impetus Turns.

As far as possible try to use right-handed and left-handed turns alternately: this will make the dance much more effective.

Impetus Turn

GENTLEMAN

Begin backing L.O.D. and finish backing diag. to centre against L.O.D.

	1. Back L.F.	Turning to R.	s.
Heel	2. Close R.F. back to L.F., turning from L. heel on to R.F.	to face diag. to centre.	
Turn	3. Side L.F. slightly back.		Q.
	4. Back R.F.		Q. s.

Amount of Turn: Make ⅜ turn to R. between 1 and 2; make ¼ turn to R. between 2 and 3.

Footwork: 1. T.H. 2. H.T. 3. T.H. 4. T.

Contrary body movement: Used on 1 and 4.

Body sway: Sway to L. on 2.

LADY

Begin facing L.O.D. and finish facing diag. to centre against L.O.D.

1. Forward R.F. }
2. Side L.F.   } Turning to R. to back diag. to centre.
3. Brush R.F. to L.F. and step diag. forward with it.
4. Forward L.F.

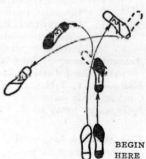

Amount of turn: Make ⅜ turn to R. between 1 and 2; make ¼ turn to R. between 2 and 3.

Footwork: 1. H.T. 2. T. 3. T.H. 4. H.

Contrary body movement: Used on 1 and 4.

Body sway: Sway to R. on 2.

This fig. may be preceded by:
(1) Three steps of the Natural Turn.
(2) Six steps of the Reverse Wave.

This fig. may be followed by:
(1) A Feather Finish danced diag. to centre or diag. to wall if the Impetus Turn is danced at a corner.
(2) Two steps of a Feather Finish, check into a Top Spin.

Note. For a Feather Finish see 5, 6 and 7 of Reverse Turn (page 64).

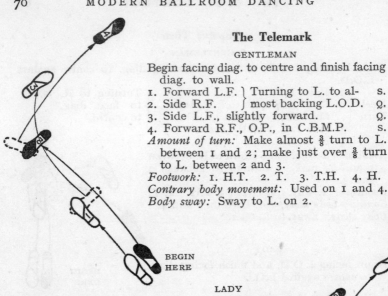

The Telemark

GENTLEMAN

Begin facing diag. to centre and finish facing
    diag. to wall.

1. Forward L.F. } Turning to L. to al-   S.
2. Side R.F. } most backing L.O.D.   Q.
3. Side L.F., slightly forward.   Q.
4. Forward R.F., O.P., in C.B.M.P.   S.

Amount of turn: Make almost ⅜ turn to L.
    between 1 and 2; make just over ⅜ turn
    to L. between 2 and 3.
Footwork: 1. H.T. 2. T. 3. T.H. 4. H.
Contrary body movement: Used on 1 and 4.
Body sway: Sway to L. on 2.

BEGIN
HERE

LADY

Begin backing diag. to centre and finish backing
    diag. to wall.

Heel
Turn
{
1. Back R.F.   } Turning to S.
2. Close L.F. to R.F., } L. to face
   turning from R. } L.O.D.
   heel on to L.F.   Q.
}
3. Side R.F. slightly back.   Q.
4. Back L.F. in C.B.M.P., P.O.   S.

Amount of turn: Make ⅜ turn to L. between 1 and
    2; make ⅜ turn to L. between 2 and 3.
Footwork: 1. T.H. 2. H.T. 3. T.H. 4. T.
Contrary body movement: Used on 1 and 4.
Body sway: Sway to R. on 2.

BEGIN
HERE

This fig. may be preceded by:
(1) The Feather Step
(2) A Change of Direction.
(3) The Reverse Wave.
(4) The Hover Feather.
(5) The Natural Hover Telemark.
(6) The Natural Telemark.
(7) The Natural Twist Turn.
(8) Any Feather Finish danced
    diag. to centre.

This fig. may be followed by:
(1) The Feather Step (last three
    steps)
(2) The Natural Turn (com-
    menced on last step of the
    Telemark, outside partner).
(3) The Natural Tele- ⎫ As for
    mark.   ⎪ Natural
(4) The   Natural ⎬ Turn
    Hover Telemark. ⎭ above.

Open Telemark (with a Feather Finish)

GENTLEMAN

Begin facing diag. to centre and finish facing diag. to wall.

1. Forward L.F. ⎞ turning to L. to back   s.
2. Side R.F. ⎠ diag. to wall.   Q.
3. Side L.F. slightly forward, in P.P.   Q.
4. Forward R.F. in P.P. and C.B.M.P.   s.

Feather ⎧ 5. Diag. forward L.F., preparing to step. outside partner in C.B.M.P.   Q.
Finish ⎨ 6. Forward R.F., O.P. in C.B.M.P.   Q.
⎩ 7. Forward L.F.   s.

Amount of turn: Make ¼ turn to L. between 1 and 2; make ½ turn to L. between 2 and 3. (Turn partner square between 4 and 5.)
Footwork: 1. H.T. 2. T. 3. T.H. 4. H.T. 5. T. 6. T.H. 7. H.
Contrary body movement: Used on 1, 4 and 7.
Body sway: Sway to L. on 2; sway to R. on 5 and 6.

LADY

Begin backing diag. to centre and finish backing diag. to wall.

1. Back R.F.   s.
Heel ⎧ 2. Close L.F. to R.F., turning ⎞ Turning to L.
Turn ⎨ from R. heel on to L.F. ⎠ to face L.O.D.   Q.
3. Diag. forward R.F. in P.P.   Q.
4. Forward L.F. and across in P.P. and C.B.M.P. s.

Feather ⎧ 5. Side R.F., slightly back.   Q.
Finish ⎨ 6. Back L.F. in C.B.M.P., P.O.   Q.
⎩ 7. Back R.F.   s.

Amount of turn: Make ⅜ turn to L. between 1 and 2; make ¼ turn to L. between 4 and 5; make ⅛ turn to L. between 5 and 6.
Footwork: 1. T.H. 2. H.T. 3. T.H. 4. H.T. 5. T.H. 6. T.H. 7. T.
Contrary body movement: Used on 1, 4 and 7.
Body sway: Sway to R. on 2; sway to L. on 5 and 6.

This fig. may be preceded by:
(1) The Feather Step.
(2) The Hover Feather.
(3) The Natural Telemark.
(4) The Natural Hover Telemark.
(5) The Natural Twist Turn.
(6) The Top Spin ended diag. to centre.
(7) Any Feather Finish ended diag. to centre.

This fig. may be followed by:
(1) The Feather Finish as above (steps 5, 6 and 7).
(2) The Natural Turn from fourth step.
(3) The Natural Turn to the Outside Swivel (see Outside Swivel notes).
(4) The Natural Twist Turn from fourth step.
(5) The Natural Telemark from fourth step.
(6) The Natural Hover Telemark from fourth step.

Natural Telemark

GENTLEMAN

Begin facing diag. to wall and finish facing diag. to centre.

1. Forward R.F.	⎱ Turning to R.	s.
2. Side L.F.	⎰ to face diag.	Q.
3. Side R.F. (small step)	to centre.	Q.
4. Diag. forward L.F., preparing to step outside partner.		Q.
5. Forward R.F., O.P., in C.B.M.P.		Q.
6. Forward L.F.		s.

Amount of turn: Make ¼ turn to R. between 1 and 2; make ½ turn to R. between 2 and 3.
Footwork: 1. H.T. 2. T. 3. T. 4. T. 5. T.H. 6. H.
Contrary body movement: Used on 1 and 6.
Body sway: Sway to R. on 2; sway to L. on 4.

Note. At a corner ½ turn to R. will be made between 1 and 3.

LADY

Begin backing diag. to wall and finish backing diag. to centre.

	1. Back L.F.	⎱ Turning to R.	s.
Heel	2. Close R.F. to L.F., turning from L. heel onto R.F.	⎰ to face L.O.D.	
Turn			Q.
	3. Side L.F., and R.F. brushes towards L.F.		Q.
	4. Diag. back R.F.		Q.
	5. Back L.F., in C.B.M.P., P.O.		Q.
	6. Back R.F.		s.

Amount of turn: Make ⅜ turn between 1 and 2; make ⅜ turn between 2 and 3.
Footwork: 1. T.H. 2. H.T. 3. T. 4. T.H. 5. T.H. 6. T.
Contrary body movement: Used on 1 and 6.
Body sway: Sway to L. on 2; sway to R. on 4.

This fig. may be preceded by:
(1) The Three Step.
(2) The Telemark, making last step the first of the Natural Telemark.
(3) The Open Telemark, making last step the first of the Natural Telemark.

This fig. may be followed by:
(1) Any Reverse fig. (i.e. the Reverse Turn, the Telemark the Open Telemark).

Hover Telemark

GENTLEMAN

Begin facing diag. to wall and finish facing diag. to centre.

1. Forward L.F.
2. Side R.F. and brush L.F. towards R.F.
3. Side L.F., slightly forward.
4. Forward R.F., O.P., in C.B.M.P.

} Turning to L. to diag. to centre.

s.
Q.
Q.
s.

Amount of turn: Make ¼ turn to L. between 1 and 3.
Footwork: 1. H.T. 2. T. of R.F., then inside edge of T. of L.F.
    3. T.H. 4. H.
Contrary body movement: Used on 1 and 4.
Body sway: Sway to L. on 2.

LADY

Begin backing diag. to wall and finish backing diag. to centre.

1. Back R.F.
2. Side L.F. and brush R.F. towards L.F.
3. Side R.F., slightly back.
4. Back L.F., in C.B.M.P., P.O.

} Turning to L. to back diag. to centre.

s.
Q.
Q.
s.

Amount of turn: Make ¼ turn to L. between 1 and 3.
Footwork: 1. T.H. 2. T. of L.F., then inside edge of T. of R.F.
    3. T.H. 4. T.
Contrary body movement: Used on 1 and 4.
Body sway: Sway to R. on 2.

This fig. may be preceded by:
(1) The Feather Step.
(2) The Reverse Turn or any Feather Finish ended diag. to wall.
(3) The Weave.
(4) The Top Spin.

This fig. may be followed by:
(1) The Feather Step (steps 2, 3 and 4).
(2) The Natural Turn; the Natural Telemark; the Natural Hover Telemark (if the Hover Telemark is danced near a corner and ended diag. to wall of new L.O.D.).

Hover Feather

The Hover Feather is introduced as an alternative ending to the Natural Turn, or the Reverse Wave; it is also used as an ending to the Natural Hover Telemark and the Natural Twist Turn.

(It is described after the fourth step of the Natural Turn.)

GENTLEMAN

Begin with back to L.O.D., after 1, 2, 3 and 4 of the Natural Turn, and finish diag. to centre.

	1. Dance a Heel Pull (turning to face diag. to centre).	Q.	or s.
	2. Rising on R.F. to toes, brush L.F. slightly towards R.F.	Q.	
Hover Feather	3. Diag. forward L.F., preparing to step outside partner.	Q.	
	4. Forward R.F., O.P., in C.B.M.P.	Q.	
	5. Forward L.F. (in front of partner).	S.	

Amount of Turn: Nil after the Heel Pull, which finishes diag. to centre.

Footwork on Hover Feather: 3. T.   4. T.H.   5. H.

Contrary body movement: Used on 5.

Body sway: Sway to L. on 1, 2 and 3.

Note. In standard technique, steps 1 and 2 are timed as one "slow".

This fig. may be preceded by:
(1) Any Heel Pull (i.e., five steps of the Natural Turn or eight steps of the Reverse Wave).
(2) The Hover Feather is used as part of the Natural Twist Turn and the Natural Hover Telemark.

This fig. may be followed by:
(1) The Reverse Turn.
(2) The Open Telemark.
(3) The Closed Telemark.
(4) The Box.
(5) The Change of Direction. (If the Hover Feather is danced near a corner it would end diag. to new wall.)
(6) The Three Step (if the Hover Feather is danced near a corner).

Hover Feather

LADY

Begin facing L.O.D., after 1, 2, 3 and 4 of the Natural Turn, and finish back diag. to centre.

	1. Side L.F.	Q.	} or s.
	2. Rising on L.F., brush R.F. towards L.F.	Q.	
Hover	3. Diag. back R.F.	Q.	
Feather	4. Back L.F., in C.B.M.P., P.O.	Q.	
	5. Back R.F. (partner in front).	S.	

Amount of turn: Nil, after the first step, which finishes backing diag. to centre.

Footwork on Hover Feather: 1. T.H. 2. T.H. 3. T.

Contrary body movement: Used on 5.

Body sway: Sway to R. on 1, 2 and 3.

For preceding and following figs. for the Hover Feather, see below the description of gentleman's steps.

Natural Hover Telemark

GENTLEMAN

Begin facing diag. to wall and finish facing diag. to centre.

	1. Forward R.F.	Turning to R. to back	S.
	2. Side L.F.	diag. to centre.	Q.
Heel	3. Pull R.F. back to side of L.F., turning		
Pull	from heel of L.F. onto R.F., feet slightly apart.		Q.
	4. L. knee veers towards R.		S.
Hover	5. Diag. forward L.F., preparing to step O.P.		Q.
Feather	6. Forward R.F., O.P., in C.B.M.P.		Q.
	7. Forward L.F. (in front of partner).		S.

Amount of turn: Make ¼ turn to R. between 1 and 2; make ½ turn to R. between 2 and 3.

Footwork: 1. H.T. 2. T.H. 3. H., inside edge of foot, whole foot. 4. T. of R.F., pressure on inside edge of T. of L.F. 5. T. 6. T.H. 7. H.

Contrary body movement: Used on 1 and 7.

Body sway: Sway to R. on 2; sway to L. on 3, 4 and 5.

This fig. may be preceded by:
(1) The Three Step.
(2) The Telemark (making the last step of the Telemark the first of the Natural Hover Telemark).
(3) The Open Telemark (as from the Telemark).

This fig. may be followed by:
(1) Any Reverse fig.

Natural Hover Telemark

LADY

Begin backing diag. to wall and finish backing diag. to centre.

Heel Turn	1. Back L.F.	Turning to R. to face L.O.D.	S.
	2. Close R.F. to L.F., turning from L. heel onto R.F.		Q.
	3. Side L.F.		Q.
	4. Brush R.F. to L.F.		S.
Hover Feather	5. Diag. back R.F.		Q.
	6. Back L.F., in C.B.M.P., P.O.		Q.
	7. Back R.F. (partner in front).		S.

Amount of turn: Make ⅜ turn to R. between 1 and 2; make ⅜ turn to R. between 2 and 3.
Footwork: 1. T.H. 2. H.T. 3. T. 4. T. of L.F. and inside edge of T. of R.F. 5. T.H. 6. T.H. 7. T.
Contrary body movement: Used on 1 and 7.
Body sway: Sway to L. on 2; sway to R. on 3, 4 and 5.
For preceding and following figs. for the Natural Hover Telemark see below the description of gentleman's steps.

Natural Twist Turn

GENTLEMAN

Begin facing L.O.D. and finish facing diag. to centre.

	1. Forward R.F.	Turning to R. to back diag. to centre.	S.
	2. Side L.F.		Q.
	3. Cross R.F. behind L.F., slightly back.		"and"
	4. Twist to R. on heel of L.F. and toe of R.F. (to face diag. to centre).		Q.
	5. Rise up on to toes, as in the Hover Feather.		S.
Hover Feather	6. Diag. forward L.F., preparing to step O.P.		Q.
	7. Forward R.F., O.P., in C.B.M.P.		Q.
	8. Forward L.F. (in front of partner).		S.

Amount of turn: Make ½ turn to R. between 1 and 3; make ⅜ turn to R. on the twist.

Footwork: 1. H.T.   2. T.H.   3. T.   4. Twist on T. of R.F. and H. of L.F. with feet flat (end with weight on R.F.).   5. T. of R.F., with pressure on inside edge of T. of L.F.   6. T.   7. T.H.   8. H.

Contrary body movement: Used on 1 and 8.

Body sway: Sway to R. on 2 and 3; sway to L. on 5 and 6.

This fig. may be preceded by:	*This fig. may be followed by:*
(1) The Three Step.	(1) Any Reverse fig.
(2) The Telemark.	
(3) The Open Telemark.	

Natural Twist Turn

LADY

Begin backing L.O.D. and finish backing diag. to centre.

	1. Back L.F.	⎫ Turning to	s.
Heel	2. Close R.F. to L.F., turning	⎬ R. to face	
Turn	from L. heel onto R.F.	⎭ L.O.D.	Q.
	3. Forward L.F., preparing to step O.P.		"and"
	4. Forward R.F., O.P., in C.B.M.P.		Q.
	5. Side L.F., and brush R.F. towards L.F.		s.
Hover	6. Diag. back R.F.		Q.
Feather	7. Back L.F., in C.B.M.P., P.O.		Q.
	8. Back R.F. (partner in front).		s.

Amount of turn: Make ½ turn to R. between 1 and 2; make ⅛ turn to R. between 2 and 4; make ¼ turn to R. between 4 and 5.

Footwork: 1. T.H.   2. H.T.   3. T.   4. T.   5. T., and inside edge of T. of R.F.   6. T.H.   7. T.H.   8. T.

Contrary body movement: Used on 1, 4 and 8.

Body sway: Sway to L. on 2 and 3; sway to R. on 5 and 6.

For preceding and following figs. for the Natural Twist Turn see below the description of gentleman's steps.

Top Spin

GENTLEMAN

At a corner, begin facing diag. to wall and finish facing diag. to centre of new L.O.D.

	1. Back on to L.F., in C.B.M.P., P.O.	Q.
	2. Back R.F. (partner in front).	Q.

5, 6, 7 of the Reverse Turn	{	3. Side L.F., slightly forward.	Q.
		4. Forward R.F., O.P., in C.B.M.P.	Q.
		5. Forward L.F. (in front of partner).	S.

Amount of turn: Make ¼ turn to L. between 1 and 2; make ¼ turn to L. between 2 and 3.

Footwork: 1. T.   2. T.   3. T.   4. T.H.   5. H.

Contrary body movement: Used on 2 and 5.

Body sway: Sway to R. on 3 and 4.

This fig. may be preceded by:	*This fig. may be followed by:*
(1) Six steps of the Reverse Turn.	(1) Any Reverse fig. (i.e., the
(2) Three steps of a Feather Step at a corner, danced diag. to wall.	Reverse Turn, the Telemark, the Open Telemark).
(3) Six steps of the Weave.	

Top Spin

LADY

At a corner begin backing diag. to wall and finish backing diag. to centre of new L.O.D.

| | 1. Forward R.F., O.P., in C.B.M.P. | Q. |
| | 2. Forward L.F. (in front of partner). | Q. |

5, 6, 7 of the Reverse Turn	{	3. Side R.F.	Q.
		4. Back L.F., in C.B.M.P., P.O.	Q.
		5. Back R.F. (partner in front).	S.

Amount of turn: Make ¼ turn to L. between 1 and 2; make ¼ turn to L. between 2 and 4.

Footwork: 1. T.   2. T.   3. T.H.   4. T.H.   5. T.

Contrary body movement: Used on 2 and 5.

Body sway: Sway to L. on 3 and 4.

For preceding and following figs. for the Top Spin see below the description of gentleman's steps.

Outside Swivel

Note. This figure is preceded by the Open Telemark making only half a turn to L. on it, followed by 1, 2 and 3 of the Natural Turn commenced in P.P. making a quarter of a turn to R.

GENTLEMAN

Begin backing diag. to wall and finish facing diag. to centre.

1. Back L.F. in C.B.M.P., P.O.	Q.	
2. Cross R.F. loosely in front of L.F., swivelling partner into P.P. (without weight).	Q.	} or s.
3. Forward R.F. and across in P.P. and C.B.M.P.	S.	

Follow with the Feather Finish taken diag. to centre
(turning partner square). Q.Q.S.

Amount of turn: Make ¼ turn to R. by turning toe of L.F. inwards
between 1 and 2.

Footwork: 1. T.H. 2. Pressure on T. of R.F. 3. H.T., Feather
Finish, T., T.H., H.

Contrary body movement: Used on 1 and 3.

Body sway: Nil.

Note. In standard technique steps 1 and 2 are timed as one "slow".

This fig. may be preceded by:
(1) 1, 2 and 3 of the Natural Turn
after the underturned Open
Telemark (see note above).

This fig. may be followed by:
(1) The Feather Finish.
(2) The Outside Swivel, danced
without any turn at a corner,
and the following Feather
Finish danced diag. to new
centre.

(3) The Outside Swivel, danced
without any turn, on the sides
of the room, when it would be
followed by a Feather Finish
danced diag. to centre against
L.O.D., into a Top Spin,
making ½ turn to L. to end
diag. to wall.
(4) The Weave, when no turn is
made on the Swivel.

Outside Swivel

LADY

Begin facing diag. to wall and finish backing diag. to centre.

1. Forward R.F., O.P., in C.B.M.P. Q.
2. Close L.F. to R.F., slightly back, without weight,   } or S.
opening to P.P. Q.
3. Forward L.F. and across in P.P. and C.B.M.P. S.

Follow with the Feather Finish diag. to centre (turning
square to partner). Q.Q.S.

Amount of turn: Make ½ turn to R. between 1 and 2.

Footwork: 1. H.T.H. 2. Pressure on inside edge of T. of L.F.
3. H.T., Feather Finish, T.H., T.H., T.

Contrary body movement: Used on 1 and 3.

Body sway: Nil.

Note. If the Outside Swivel is used at a corner the lady turns slightly
less and the gentleman makes no turn.

For preceding and following figs. for the Outside Swivel see below
the description of gentleman's steps.

The Weave

GENTLEMAN

Begin facing diag. to centre, against L.O.D., and finish facing diag. to wall.

1. Forward on to L.F.	Turning to L.	Q.
2. Side R.F.	to back diag.	Q.
3. Back L.F., in C.B.M.P., P.O.	to centre.	Q.
4. Back R.F. (partner in front).		Q.
Feather Finish { 5. Side and slightly forward with L.F.		Q.
6. Forward R.F., O.P., in C.B.M.P.		Q.
7. Forward L.F. (in front of partner).		S.

Amount of turn: Make ¼ turn to L. between 1 and 3; make ¼ turn to L. between 4 and 5.
Footwork: 1. H.T. 2. T. 3. T. 4. T. 5. T. 6. T.H. 7. H.
Contrary body movement: Used on 1, 4 and 7.
Body sway: Sway to L. on 2 and 3; sway to R. on 5 and 6.

This fig. may be preceded by:
(1) Four steps of the Reverse Wave.
(2) Four steps of the Reverse Turn, when the Weave will commence backing L.O.D., and less turn made on it between 1 and 3 unless danced at a corner.
(3) The Outside Swivel, danced without turning on swivel (Lady will be turned square at end of 3 of the Outside Swivel into the Weave).

This fig. may be followed by:
(1) The Three Step.
(2) The Change of Direction.
(3) The Wave (commenced diag. to wall, making ½ turn to L. between 1 and 3 of Wave).
(4) The Hover Telemark.
(5) The Box (commenced diag. to wall, making ⅜ turn to L. between 1 and 2 of the Box).

LADY

Begin backing diag. to centre, against L.O.D., and finish backing diag. to wall.

1. Back on to R.F.	Turning to L.	Q.
2. Side L.F.	to face diag.	Q.
3. Forward R.F., O.P., in C.B.M.P.	to centre.	Q.
4. Forward L.F. (in front of partner).		Q.
Feather Finish { 5. Side R.F., still turning.		Q.
6. Back L.F., in C.B.M.P., P.O.		Q.
7. Back R.F. (partner in front).		S.

Amount of turn: Make ¼ turn to L. between 1 and 2; make ¼ turn
to L. between 4 and 6.
Footwork: 1. T.H.   2. T.   3. T.   4. T.   5. T.H.   6. T.H.   7. T.
Contrary body movement: Used on 1, 4 and 7.
Body sway: Sway to R. on 2 and 3; sway to L. on 5 and 6.
For preceding and following figs. for the Weave see below the
description of gentleman's steps.

The Box

GENTLEMAN

Begin facing L.O.D. and finish facing diag. to centre against L.O.D.

1. Forward L.F.	⎫ Turning to	s.	
2. Side R.F.	⎬ L. to back-	q.	⎫ or s.
3. Close L.F. to R.F. (weight on R.F.).	⎭ ing wall.	q.	⎭
4. Back L.F., in C.B.M.P., P.O.		s.	
5. Back R.F. (partner in front).		q.	
6. Side L.F., slightly forward.		q.	
7. Forward R.F., O.P., in C.B.M.P.		s.	

Amount of turn: Make ¼ turn to L. between 1 and 3; make ⅛ turn
to L. between 5 and 6.
Footwork: 1. H.T.   2. T.H.   3. Inside edge of T. of L.F.   4. T.H.
5. T.   6. T.H.   7. H.
Contrary body movement: Used on 1, slightly on 5, and on 7.
Body sway: Nil.

Note. In standard technique, steps 2 and 3 are timed as one "slow".

This fig. may be preceded by:
(1) The Feather Step.
(2) The Reverse Turn (when the
Box will commence diag. to
wall and more turn made to
L. between 1 and 2).
(3) The Hover Feather (when less
turn will be made between 1
and 2 of the Box).

(4) The Top Spin or any Feather
Finish (when amount of turn
between 1 and 2 of the Box
will be the same as No. 2).

This fig. may be followed by:
(1) The Feather Step curved to
R., to end diag. to centre.
(2) The Weave.

The Box

LADY

Begin backing L.O.D., and finish backing diag. to centre against
   L.O.D.

1. Back R.F.	⎫ Turning to	s. ⎫
2. Side L.F.	⎬ L. to face	Q. ⎬ or s.
3. Close R.F. to L.F. (weight on L.F.).	⎭ wall.	Q. ⎭
4. Forward R.F., O.P., in C.B.M.P.		s.
5. Forward L.F. (in front of partner).		Q.
6. Side R.F., slightly back.		Q.
7. Back L.F., in C.B.M.P., P.O.		s.

Amount of turn: Make ¼ turn to L. between 1 and 3; make ⅛ turn
   to L. between 5 and 6.

Footwork: 1. T.H.   2. T.H.   3. Inside edge of T. of R.F.   4. H.T.
   5. T.   6. T.H.   7. T.

Contrary body movement: Used on 1, slightly on 5, and on 7.

Body sway: Nil.

Natural Zig-Zag

A very useful figure when you are too close to the wall to dance a
full Natural Turn.

GENTLEMAN

Begin facing diag. to wall and finish facing diag. to wall.

1, 2. Dance 1 and 2 of the Natural Turn (turning to R. to back diag. to centre).	s.Q.
3. Back R.F.	Q.
4, 5, 6. Dance 5, 6 and 7 of Reverse Turn (Feather Finish).	Q.Q.s.

Amount of turn: Make ¼ turn to R. between 1 and 2; make ¼ turn
   to L. between 3 and 4.

Footwork: 1. H.T.   2. T.   3. T.   4. T.   5. T.H.   6. H.

Contrary body movement: Used on 1, 3 and 6.

Body sway: Sway to R. on 4 and 5.

This fig. may be preceded by:	*This fig. may be followed by:*
(1) The Three Step.	(1) The Three Step.
(2) The Telemark, making last step of the Telemark first of the Natural Zig-Zag.	(2) The Reverse Wave.
	(3) The Change of Direction.
	(4) The Box.
	(5) The Hover Telemark.
	(6) The Top Spin after fifth step of the Natural Zig-Zag.

Natural Zig-Zag

LADY

Begin backing diag. to wall and finish backing diag. to wall.

1, 2. Dance 1 and 2 of the Natural Turn (turning
    to R. to face diag. to centre).   S.Q.
3. Forward L.F.   Q.
4, 5, 6. Dance 5, 6 and 7 of Reverse Turn (Feather
    Finish).   Q.Q.S.

Amount of turn: Make $\frac{1}{4}$ turn to R. between 1 and 2; make $\frac{1}{4}$ turn
to L. between 3 and 5.
Footwork: 1. T.H. 2. H.T. 3. T. 4. T.H. 5. T.H. 6. T.
Contrary body movement: Used on 1, 3 and 6.
Body sway: Sway to L. on 4 and 5.
For preceding and following figs. see below the description of
gentleman's steps.

Natural Weave

GENTLEMAN

Begin and finish facing diag. to wall.

1, 2. Dance 1 and 2 of the Natural Turn (turning
    to back diag. to centre).   S.Q.
3. Back R.F.   Q.
4. Back L.F., in C.B.M.P., P.O.   Q.
5. Back R.F., partner in front.   Q.
6, 7, 8. Dance 5, 6 and 7 of Reverse Turn (Feather
    Finish).   Q.Q.S.

Amount of turn: Make $\frac{1}{4}$ turn to R. between 1 and 2; make $\frac{1}{4}$ turn
to L. between 5 and 6.
Footwork: 1. H.T. 2. T. 3. T. 4. T. 5. T. 6. T. 7. T.H. 8. H.
Contrary body movement: Used on 1, 5 and 8.
Body sway: Sway to R. on 2 and 3; sway to R. on 6 and 7.

This fig. may be preceded by:
(1) The Three Step.
(2) The Telemark, making last
    step of the Telemark first of
    the Natural Weave.

This fig. may be followed by:
(1) The Three Step.
(2) The Reverse Wave.
(3) The Change of Direction.
(4) The Box.
(5) The Hover Telemark.
(6) The Top Spin after seventh
    step of the Natural Weave.

Natural Weave

LADY

Begin backing diag. to wall and finish backing diag. to wall.

1, 2. Dance 1 and 2 of the Natural Turn (turning
      to face diag. to centre).   S.Q.

3. Forward L.F.   Q.

4. Forward R.F., O.P., in C.B.M.P.   Q.

5. Forward L.F. (in front of partner).   Q.

6, 7, 8. Dance 5, 6 and 7 of the Reverse Turn
      (Feather Finish).   Q.Q.S.

Amount of turn: Make ¼ turn to R. between 1 and 2; make ¼ turn
    to L. between 5 and 7.

Footwork: 1. T.H. 2. H.T. 3. T. 4. T. 5. T. 6. T.H. 7. T.H.
    8. T.

Contrary body movement: Used on 1, 5 and 8.

Body sway: Sway to L. on 2 and 3; sway to L. on 6 and 7.

For preceding and following figs. see beneath the description of
    gentleman's steps.

CHAPTER VIII

THE QUICKSTEP

SOME GENERAL NOTES

THE music of the Quickstep is undoubtedly the most popular dance music today.

It is danced to the same music as Quick Rhythm, but played in stricter tempo. If the band plays a very fast tempo, you will find it difficult to dance the Quickstep correctly, and in this event you will find it advisable to dance Quick Rhythm instead.

You can always mix Quickstep with Quick Rhythm, even when the band is playing a steady tempo. If when dancing the Quickstep you find yourself temporarily in a crowd, drop into Quick Rhythm and then go back to Quickstep when you find a clear space.

There are two fundamental movements in this dance, the walk and the Chassé, and all the basic figures are built up on these two movements.

The walk forward is the same as in the Slow Foxtrot, only danced quicker.

The walk backward is also the same as in the Slow Foxtrot, only danced quicker.

The Chassés may be danced in different ways, but they are always made up of three steps counted " quick, quick, slow", and take four beats of the music. The feet are closed together on the second of the three steps. In the different figures where they are used, they are clearly described.

The Hold is the same as described on page 20.

Quarter Turns

This is the most important figure in the Quickstep. It is called the Quarter Turns because usually a quarter turn to R. is made on the first part, and a quarter turn to L. on the last part.

Quarter Turns

GENTLEMAN

Begin and finish facing diag. to wall.

	1. Forward R.F.	Turning to R.	s.
Chassé	2. Side L.F.	to back diag.	Q.
	3. Close R.F. to L.F.	to centre.	Q.
	4. Side L.F., slightly back.		s.
	5. Back R.F., turning to L.		s.
Heel	6. Close L.F. to R.F., turning		Q.
Pivot	7. to L. on R. heel		Q.
	8. Forward L.F.		s.

Amount of turn: Make ¼ turn to R. between 1 and 3; make ¼ turn to L. between 5 and 7.

If the Quarter Turns are preceded by a figure which ends facing L.O.D., make ⅜ turn to R. between 1 and 3; if to be followed by a reverse figure, make ⅜ turn to L. between 5 and 7.

Footwork: 1. H.T. 2. T. 3. T. 4. T.H. 5. T.H. 6. H. 7. H. of R.F., pressure on T. of L. F. 8. H.

Contrary body movement: Used on 1, 5 and 8.

Body sway: Sway to R. on 2 and 3; sway to R. on 6 and 7.

Note. On 6 and 7 the gentleman is making one step, doing what is known as a Heel Pivot, while the lady is making two steps; that is why it is counted Q.Q.

BEGIN HERE

This fig. may be preceded by:
(1) The Chassé Reverse Turn.
(2) The Cross Chassé.
(3) The Drag.
(4) The Progressive Chassé or any fig. ended diag. to wall leaving R.F. free (lady L.F.).
(5) The Zig-Zag or Running Zig-Zag when commenced along L.O.D.
(6) The Natural Turn.
(7) The Natural Pivot Turn.
(8) The Running Right Turn.

This fig. may be followed by:
(1) Any Natural fig. when ended diag. to wall.
(2) The Cross Chassé.
(3) The Drag.
(4) The Change of Direction.
(5) The Cross Swivel.
(6) Any Reverse figure when ended along L.O.D.
(7) The Progressive Chassé after the first four steps. (Very popular.)

Quarter Turns

LADY

Begin and finish backing diag. to wall.

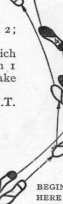

Chassé
1. Back L.F.	Turning to R. to	S.
2. Side R.F.	face diag. to centre.	Q.
3. Close L.F. to R.F.		Q.
4. Diag. forward R.F.		S.
5. Forward L.F.		S.
6. Side R.F.		Q.
7. Close L.F. to R.F.		Q.
8. Step back R.F.		S.

Amount of turn: Make ¼ turn to R. between 1 and 2; make ¼ turn to L. between 5 and 7.

If the Quarter Turns are preceded by a figure which ends along L.O.D., make ⅜ turn to R. between 1 and 2. If to be followed by a reverse figure, make ⅜ turn to L. between 5 and 7.

Footwork: 1. T.H. 2. T. 3. T. 4. T.H. 5. H.T. 6. T. 7. T.H. 8. T.

Contrary body movement: Used on 1, 5 and 8.

Body sway: Sway to L. on 2 and 3; sway to L. on 6 and 7. For preceding and following figs. for Quarter Turns see below the description of gentleman's steps.

Progressive Chassé

This figure is really an ending to several others (see below, in column of preceding figs.).

GENTLEMAN

Begin backing diag. to centre and finish facing diag. to wall.

Chassé
1. Back R.F.	Turning to L. to face diag. to wall.	S.
2. Side L.F.		Q.
3. Close R.F. to L.F.		Q.
4. Side L.F., slightly forward.		S.
5. Forward R.F., O.P., in C.B.M.P.		S.

Amount of turn: Make ¼ turn to L. between 1 and 2.

Footwork: 1. T.H. 2. T. 3. T. 4. T.H. 5. H.

Contrary body movement: Used on 1 and 5.

Body sway: Nil.

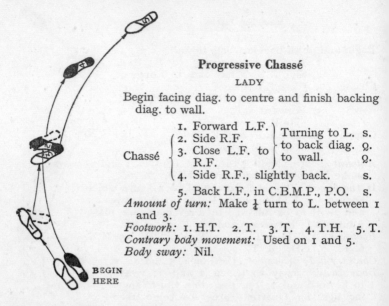

Progressive Chassé

LADY

Begin facing diag. to centre and finish backing diag. to wall.

Chassé
1. Forward L.F. ⎫ Turning to L. s.
2. Side R.F.   ⎪ to back diag. Q.
3. Close L.F. to ⎬ to wall.   Q.
   R.F.   ⎪
4. Side R.F., slightly back. ⎭ s.
5. Back L.F., in C.B.M.P., P.O.   s.

Amount of turn: Make ¼ turn to L. between 1 and 3.
Footwork: 1. H.T. 2. T. 3. T. 4. T.H. 5. T.
Contrary body movement: Used on 1 and 5.
Body sway: Nil.

BEGIN
HERE

This fig. may be preceded by:
(1) Four steps of the Quarter Turns.
(2) Three steps of the Reverse Turn.
(3) Three steps of the Chassé Reverse Turn.
(4) The Natural Spin Turn.
(5) The Impetus Turn.
(6) The Quick Open Reverse Turn.

This fig. may be followed by:
(1) Any Natural fig.
(2) The Forward Lock Step.
(3) The Fish Tail.
(4) Any Reverse fig. if turned more to L.

Note. Most good dancers use this ending to figures more than the Heel Pivot.

Lock Step Forward

This figure can be preceded by practically any figure which finishes forward with R.F. outside partner (lady—back L.F., partner outside). No. 1 described below is therefore the last step of the preceding figure.

GENTLEMAN

Begin and finish facing diag. to wall.

1. Forward R.F., O.P., in C.B.M.P.   S.
2. Diag. forward L.F.   Q.
3. Cross R.F. behind L.F.   Q.
4. Diag. forward L.F.   S.
5. Forward R.F., O.P., in C.B.M.P.   S.

Amount of turn: Nil.
Footwork: 1. H.T. 2. T. 3. T. 4. T.H. 5. H.
Contrary body movement: Used slightly on 1; used on 5.
Body sway: Nil.

Note. Although the feet are diag. to wall, the body faces a little more towards the wall throughout this fig.

LADY

Begin and finish backing diag. to wall.

1. Back L.F., in C.B.M.P., P.O.   S.
2. Back R.F.   Q.
3. Cross L.F. in front of R.F.   Q.
4. Diag. back R.F.   S.
5. Back L.F., in C.B.M.P., P.O.   S.

Amount of turn: Nil.
Footwork: 1. T.H. 2. T. 3. T. 4. T.H. 5. T.
Contrary body movement: Used slightly on 1; used on 5.
Body sway: Nil.

Note. While gentleman dances the Lock Step Forward, the lady dances the Lock Step Backward.

This fig. may be preceded by:
(1) The Progressive Chassé.
(2) The Drag.
(3) The Cross Chassé.
(4) The Telemark.

This fig. may be followed by:
(1) The Quarter Turns.
(2) Any Natural Turn.

Natural Turn

This Natural figure is not as popular as the Natural Pivot or Spin Turn, but it is a good basic figure for the beginner because other figures have been built up from it.

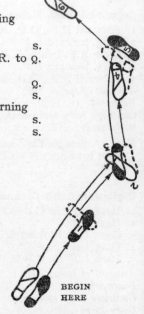

GENTLEMAN

Begin facing diag. to wall and finish facing diag. to wall of new L.O.D.

	1. Forward R.F.	} Turning to R. to back L.O.D.	s.
Chassé	2. Side L.F.		Q.
	3. Close R.F. to L.F.		Q.
	4. Back L.F.		s.
Heel Pull	5. Pull R.F. to side of L.F., turning from L. heel on to R.F.		s.
	6. Forward L.F.		s.

Amount of turn: Make ⅝ turn to R. between 1 and 3; make ⅜ turn to R. between 4 and 5.

Footwork: 1. H.T. 2. T. 3. T.H. 4. T.H. 5. H., inside edge of foot, whole foot. 6. H.

Contrary body movement: Used on 1, 4 and 6.

Body sway: Sway slightly to R. on 2 and 3.

Note. The Natural Turn, as described above, is for using round a corner. If commenced facing L.O.D., make ½ turn to R. between 1 and 3.

BEGIN
HERE

This fig. may be preceded by:
(1) Any fig. ended diag. to wall, leaving R.F. free (lady L.F.) (i.e., the Quarter Turns, the Chassé Reverse Turn, the Cross Chassé, the Drag, the Progressive Chassé, etc.).
(2) The Zig-Zag or the Running Zig-Zag (when commenced along L.O.D.).
(3) The Running Right Turn.

This fig. may be followed by:
(1) Any Natural fig. when ended diag. to wall.
(2) The Cross Chassé or the Drag (after the fifth step).

Natural Turn

LADY

Begin backing diag. to wall and finish backing diag. to wall of new L.O.D.

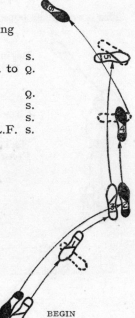

Chassé
1. Back L.F. \
2. Side R.F. | Turning to R. to s. \
3. Close L.F. to | face L.O.D. Q. \
   R.F. Q. \
4. Forward R.F. s. \
5. Side L.F. s. \
6. Back R.F., brushing it past L.F. s.

Amount of turn: Make ⅜ turn to R. between 1 and 2; make ⅜ turn to R. between 4 and 6.

Footwork: 1. T.H. 2. T. 3. T.H. 4. H.T. 5. T.H. 6. T.

Contrary body movement: Used on 1, 4 and 6.

Body sway: Sway to L. on 2 and 3.

For preceding and following figs. for Natural Turn see beneath the description of gentleman's steps.

BEGIN
HERE

Chassé Reverse Turn

This is one of the popular left-handed turns used in the Quickstep.

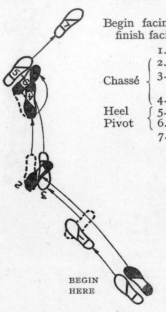

GENTLEMAN

Begin facing L.O.D., or diag. to centre, and finish facing diag. to wall.

Chassé	1. Forward L.F.	Turning to L. to back L.O.D.	s.
	2. Side R.F.		Q.
	3. Close L.F. to R.F.		Q.
	4. Back R.F.		s.
Heel Pivot	5. Close L.F. to R.F., turning to		
	6. L. on R. heel.		Q.Q.
	7. Forward L.F.		s.

Amount of turn: Make ½ or ⅜ turn to L. between 1 and 3; make ⅜ turn to L. between 4 and 6.

Footwork: 1. T.H. 2. T. 3. T.H. 4. T.H. 5. H. 6. H. of R.F., pressure on T. of L.F. 7. H.

Contrary body movement: Used on 1, 4 and 7.

Body sway: Sway to L. on 2 and 3; sway to R. on 5 and 6.

BEGIN HERE

Note. On 5 and 6 the gentleman is making one step, doing what is known as a Heel Pivot, while the lady is making two steps; that is why it is counted Q.Q.

This fig. may be preceded by:
(1) The Change of Direction.
(2) The Natural Turn ended on L.O.D
(3) The Quarter Turns.
(4) The Progressive Chassé danced diag. to centre.

This fig. may be followed by:
(1) Any Natural fig.
(2) The Cross Chassé.
(3) The Drag.
(4) The Change of Direction.
(5) The Cross Swivel.
(6) The Progressive Chassé after the first three steps. (Very popular.)

Chassé Reverse Turn

LADY

Begin backing to L.O.D., or diag. to centre, and finish backing diag. to wall.

Chassé	1. Back R.F.	Turning to	s.
	2. Side L.F.	L. to face	Q.
	3. Close R.F. to L.F.	L.O.D.	Q.
	4. Forward L.F.		s.
Chassé	5. Side R.F.		Q.
	6. Close L.F. to R.F.		Q.
	7. Back R.F.		s.

Amount of turn: Make $\frac{3}{8}$ or $\frac{1}{2}$ turn to L. between 1 and 3; make $\frac{3}{8}$ turn to L. between 4 and 6.

Footwork: 1. T.H.   2. T.   3. T.H.   4. H.T. 5. T.   6. T.H.   7. T.

Contrary body movement: Used on 1, 4 and 7.

Body sway: Sway to R. on 2 and 3; sway to L. on 5 and 6.

For preceding and following figs. for the Chassé Reverse Turn, see beneath the description of gentleman's steps.

BEGIN
HERE

Cross Chassé

GENTLEMAN

Begin and finish diag. to wall.

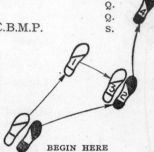

Chassé
{
1. Forward L.F.   s.
2. Side R.F. (short step).   Q.
3. Close L.F. to R.F.   Q.
4. Forward R.F., O.P., in C.B.M.P.   s.
}

Amount of turn: Nil.
Footwork: 1. H.T.   2. T.   3. T.H. 4. H.
Contrary body movement: Used on 1 and 4.
Body sway: Sway to L. on 2 and 3.

BEGIN HERE

LADY

Begin and finish backing diag. to wall.

Chassé
{
1. Back R.F.   s.
2. Side L.F. (short step).   Q.
3. Close R.F. to L.F.   Q.
4. Back L.F., in C.B.M.P., P.O.   s.
}

Amount of turn: Nil.
Footwork: 1. T.H.   2. T.   3. T.H. 4. T.
Contrary body movement: Used on 1 and 4.
Body sway: Sway lightly to R. on 2 and 3.

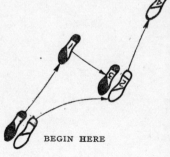

This fig. may be preceded by:
(1) The Quarter Turns or any Heel Pivot.
(2) The Double Reverse Spin.
(3) The Reverse Pivot Turn.
(4) The Natural Turn.

BEGIN HERE

This fig. may be followed by:
(1) Any Natural fig.
(2) The Quarter Turns.
(3) The Lock Step Forward.
(4) The Fish Tail.

The Zig-Zag

GENTLEMAN

Begin and finish facing L.O.D.

	1. Forward L.F.	} Turning to L. to back	s.
	2. Side R.F.	} diag. to wall.	s.
	3. Back L.F., in C.B.M.P., P.O.		s.
Heel	{ 4. Pull R.F. to side of L.F., turning from L.		
Pull	{ heel on to R.F.		s.
	5. Forward L.F.		s.

Amount of turn: Make ⅜ turn to L. between 1 and 3; make ⅜ turn to R. between 3 and 4.

Footwork: 1. H.T. 2. T.H. 3. T.H. 4. H., inside edge of foot, whole foot. 5. H.

Contrary body movement: Used on 1, 3 and 5.

Body sway: Nil.

Note. When used near a corner, make slightly less turn on 3 and 4 and finish facing diag. to wall of new L.O.D.

This fig. may be preceded by:	*This fig. may be followed by:*
(1) The Quarter Turns or any figure ending with a Heel Pivot.	(1) Any Natural fig.
	(2) The Quarter Turns.
(2) The Double Reverse Spin.	
(3) The Reverse Pivot Turn.	

LADY

Begin and finish backing L.O.D.

	1. Back R.F.	} Turning to L.	s.
Heel	{ 2. Close L.F. to R.F., turning	} to face diag.	
Turn	{ from R. heel onto L.F.	} to wall.	s.
	3. Forward R.F., O.P., in C.B.M.P.		s.
	4. Side L.F.		s.
	5. Back R.F., brushing it past L.F.		s.

Amount of turn: Make ⅜ turn to L. between 1 and 2; make ⅜ turn to R. between 3 and 5.

Footwork: 1. T.H. 2. H. 3. H.T. 4. T.H. 5. T.

Contrary body movement: Used on 1, 3 and 5.

Body sway: Nil.

Note. When used near a corner, make slightly less turn on 3, 4 and 5, and finish with back diag. to wall of new L.O.D.

For preceding and following figs. for the Zig-Zag, see below the description of gentleman's steps.

Natural Pivot Turn

This is a popular Natural Turn used in the Quickstep.

GENTLEMAN

Begin facing diag. to wall and finish the pivot facing diag. to wall of new L.O.D.

Chassé
1. Forward R.F. } Turning to L. to back L.O.D.   S.
2. Side L.F.   Q.
3. Close R.F. to L.F.   Q.
4. Back L.F., pivoting to R. (keeping R.F. in front of you in C.B.M.P.).   S.
5. Forward on to R.F.   S.

This figure is usually followed by the Quarter Turns, so 5 described above would be 1 of the Quarter Turns.

Amount of turn: Make ⅜ turn to R. between 1 and 3; make ⅜ turn on 4.
Footwork: 1. H.T.   2. T.   3. T.H.   4. T.H.T.   5. H.
Contrary body movement: Used on 1 and 4.
Body sway: Sway to R. on 2 and 3.

Note. The Natural Pivot Turn as described above is for use at a corner. If commenced facing L.O.D., make ½ turn to R. between 1 and 3.

This fig. may be preceded by:
(1) Any fig. ended diag. to wall, leaving R.F. (lady L.F.) free.
(2) Preceded by the Zig-Zag or the Running Zig-Zag when commenced along L.O.D.
(3) The Running Right Turn.

This fig. may be followed by:
(1) The Quarter Turns.
(2) The Natural Spin.

Natural Pivot Turn

LADY

Begin backing diag. to wall and finish with back diag. to wall of new L.O.D.

Chassé
{
1. Back L.F.
2. Side R.F.
3. Close L.F. to R.F.
4. Forward R.F., keeping L.F. behind you.
5. Back on to L.F.
}

Turning to R. to face L.O.D.

s.
Q.
Q.
s.
s.

This figure is usually followed by the Quarter Turns, so 5 described above would be 1 of the Quarter Turns.

Amount of turn: Make ⅜ turn to R. between 1 and 2; make ⅜ turn to R. on 4.
Footwork: 1. T.H. 2. T. 3. T.H. 4. H.T.H.
Contrary body movement: Used on 1, 4 and 5.
Body sway: Sway to L. on 2 and 3.

For preceding and following figs. for the Natural Pivot Turn, see below the description of gentleman's steps.

Note. The Natural Pivot Turn as described above is for use at a corner. If commenced backing L.O.D., make ½ turn to R. between 1 and 3.

Natural Spin Turn

GENTLEMAN

Begin facing diag. to wall and finish backing diag. to centre of new L.O.D. (described for use at a corner).

1, 2, 3, 4. Do 1, 2, 3 and 4 of the Natural Pivot Turn.

s.Q.Q.s.

Spin
{
5. Forward on to R.F., in C.B.M.P.
6. Side L.F., slightly back.
}

Q.
s.

Amount of turn: 1, 2, 3 and 4 as for Natural Pivot Turn; make ¼ turn to R. between 5 and 6.
Footwork: 1, 2, 3 and 4 as for the Natural Pivot Turn. 5. H.T. 6. T.H.
Contrary body movement: Used on 1, 4 and 5.
Body sway: 1, 2, 3 and 4 as in the Natural Pivot Turn; no sway on 5 and 6.

D

Natural Spin Turn

LADY

Begin backing diag. to wall and finish facing diag. to centre of new
L.O.D. (described for use at a corner).

1, 2, 3, 4. Do 1, 2, 3 and 4 of the Natural Pivot
                 Turn.   s.q.q.s.

Spin { 5. Back L.F., slightly to L.   s.
      { 6. Brush R.F. to L.F. and step diag. forward
           with it.   s.

Amount of turn: 1, 2, 3 and 4 as for the Natural Pivot Turn; make
   ¼ turn to R. between 5 and 6.

Footwork: 1, 2 and 3 as for the Natural Pivot Turn. 4. H.T. 5. T.
   6. T.H.

Contrary body movement: Used on 1 and 4. (The lady loses C.B.M.
   on 5.)

Body sway: 1, 2 and 3 as in the Natural Pivot Turn; no sway on
   4, 5 and 6.

This fig. may be preceded by:
(1) Any fig. ended diag. to wall,
    leaving R.F. (lady L.F.) free.
(2) The Zig-Zag or the Running
    Zig-Zag, when the Natural
    Spin Turn will commence
    along L.O.D. and more turn
    will be made on 1, 2 and 3.
(3) The Running Right Turn.

This fig. may be followed by:
(1) The last four steps of the
    Quarter Turns.
(2) A Reverse Pivot (like fourth
    step of the Reverse Pivot
    Turn).
(3) The Progressive Chassé.
(4) The Corté.

Running Zig-Zag

GENTLEMAN

Begin and finish facing L.O.D.

1. Forward L.F. } Turning to L. S.
2. Side R.F., slightly back. } to back wall. S.

Running Finish
3. Back L.F., in C.B.M.P., P.O. Q.
4. Side R.F., slightly forward. Q.
5. Forward L.F., preparing to step O.P. S.
6. Forward R.F., O.P., in C.B.M.P. S.

Amount of turn: Make ¼ turn to L. between 1 and 2; make ¼ turn to R. between 3 and 4.

Footwork: 1. H.T. 2. T.H. 3. T. 4. T. 5. T.H. 6. H.

Contrary body movement: Used on 1, 3 and 6.

Body sway: Sway to L. on 4 and 5.

BEGIN HERE

LADY

Begin and finish backing L.O.D.

Heel
Turn
{ 1. Back R.F. S.
2. Close L.F. to R.F., turning from R. heel onto L.F. } Turning to L. to face diag. to wall. S.

Running
Finish
{ 3. Forward R.F., O.P., in C.B.M.P. Q.
4. Side L.F. Q.
5. Back R.F. S.
6. Back L.F., in C.B.M.P., P.O. S.

Amount of turn: Make ⅜ turn to L. between 1 and 2; make ⅜ turn to R. between 3 and 5.

Footwork: 1. T.H. 2. H. 3. H.T. 4. T. 5. T.H. 6. T.

Contrary body movement: Used on 1, 3 and 6.

Body sway: Sway to R. on 4 and 5.

Note. Nos. 3, 4, 5 and 6 are known as the Running Finish.

BEGIN HERE

This fig. may be preceded by:
(1) The Quarter Turns or any Heel Pivot.
(2) The Double Reverse Spin, ended on L.O.D.
(3) The Reverse Pivot Turn.

This fig. may be followed by.
(1) Any Natural fig.
(2) The Lock Step forward.
(3) The Fish Tail.

Lock Step Backward

GENTLEMAN

Begin and finish backing diag. to wall.

1. Back L.F., in C.B.M.P., P.O.   s.
2. Back R.F.   Q.
3. Cross L.F. in front of R.F.   Q.
4. Diag. back R.F.   s.
5. Back L.F., in C.B.M.P., P.O.   s.

Amount of turn: Nil.
Footwork: 1. T.H.   2. T.   3. T.   4. T.H.   5. T.
Contrary body movement: Used slightly on 1; used on 5.
Body sway: Nil.

LADY

Begin and finish facing diag. to wall.

1. Forward R.F., O.P., in C.B.M.P.   s.
2. Diag. forward L.F.   Q.
3. Cross R.F. behind L.F.   Q.
4. Diag. forward L.F.   s.
5. Forward R.F., O.P., in C.B.M.P.   s.

Amount of turn: Nil.
Footwork: 1. H.T.   2. T.   3. T.   4. T.H.   5. H.
Contrary body movement: Used slightly on 1; used on 5.
Body sway: Nil.

This fig. may be preceded by:
(1) 1 and 2 of the Zig-Zag.

This fig. may be followed by:
(1) A Heel Pull (gentleman).
(2) The Running Finish (see the Running Zig-Zag note).
(3) The Impetus or the Open Impetus Turn.

The Corté

GENTLEMAN

Begin backing diag. to centre and finish facing diag. to wall.

1. Back R.F.	⎫	s.
2, 3. Close L.F. to R.F., slightly forward, weight on R.F.	⎬ Turning to L. to face diag. to wall.	q.q.
4. Back L.F., in C.B.M.P., P.O.		s.

Amount of turn: Make ¼ turn to L. between 1 and 2.
Footwork: 1. T.H. 2. H. of L.F. 3. H. of R.F., pressure on inside edge of T. of L.F. 4. T.
Contrary body movement: Used on 1 and 4.
Body sway: Sway to R. on 2 and 3.

LADY

Begin facing diag. to centre and finish facing diag. to centre against L.O.D.

	1. Forward L.F.	⎫	s.
Chassé	2. Side R.F.	⎬ Turning to L. to face diag. to centre against L.O.D.	q.
	3. Close L.F. to R.F.		q.
	4. Forward R.F., O.P., in C.B.M.P.		s.

Amount of turn: Make ¼ turn to L. between 1 and 3.
Footwork: 1. H.T. 2. T. 3. T.H. 4. H.
Contrary body movement: Used on 1 and 4.
Body sway: Sway to L. on 2 and 3.

This fig. may be preceded by:
(1) 1, 2, 3 and 4 of the Quarter Turns.
(2) 1, 2 and 3 of the Chassé Reverse Turns.
(3) The Natural Spin Turn.
(4) The Impetus Turn.
(5) The Quick Open Reverse Turn.

This fig. may be followed by:
(1) Check forward onto R.F. into the Quarter Turns, or any Natural Turn.
(2) The Running Finish.

Cross Swivel

GENTLEMAN

Begin facing diag. to wall and finish facing diag. to centre.

1. Forward L.F.	⎫ Turning to L.	s.
2. Close R.F. to L.F., slightly back, weight on L.F.	⎬ to face diag. to centre.	s.
3. Forward R.F., O.P., in C.B.M.P.	⎭	s.

Amount of turn: Make ¼ turn to L. between 1 and 2.
Footwork: 1. H. 2. Pressure on T. of L.F., foot flat and pressure on inside edge of T. of R.F. 3. H.
Contrary body movement: Used on 1 and 3.
Body sway: Sway to L. on 2.

LADY

Begin backing diag. to wall and finish backing diag. to centre.

1. Back R.F.	⎫ Turning to L.	s.
2. Close L.F. to R.F., slightly forward, weight on R.F.	⎬ to back diag. to centre.	s.
3. Back L.F., in C.B.M.P., P.O.	⎭	s.

Amount of turn: Make ¼ turn to L. between 1 and 2.
Footwork: 1. T.H. 2. H., then inside edge of T. 3. T.
Contrary body movement: Used on 1 and 3.
Body sway: Sway to R. on 2.

This fig. may be preceded by:
(1) Any Heel Pivot.
(2) The Double Reverse Spin.
(3) The Reverse Pivot.

This fig. may be followed by:
(1) The Running Finish.
(2) The Fish Tail.
(3) Any Natural Turn, or the Quarter Turns if ended diag. to wall at a corner.
(4) The Lock Step Forward.

Fish Tail

GENTLEMAN

Begin facing diag. to centre and finish facing diag. to wall.

1. Forward R.F., O.P., in C.B.M.P.	⎫ Turning to R.	s.
2. Cross L.F. behind R.F.	⎬ to face diag.	Q.
3. Short step diag. forward R.F.	⎭ to wall.	Q.
4. Diag. forward L.F.		Q.
5. Cross R.F. behind L.F.		Q.
6. Diag. forward L.F.		s.
7. Forward R.F., O.P., in C.B.M.P.		s.

Amount of turn: Make ¼ turn to R. between 1 and 3.
Footwork: 1. H.T. 2. T. 3. T. 4. T. 5. T. 6. T.H. 7. H.
Contrary body movement: Used on 1 and 7.
Body sway: Sway to R. on 2.

Note: This fig. may be danced diag. to wall with no turn.

This fig. may be preceded by:	*This fig. may be followed by:*
(1) The Cross Swivel.	(1) Any Natural Turn.
(2) Any fig. ended diag. to wall with R.F. (lady L.F.) outside lady (i.e., the Cross Chassé, the Drag, the Progressive Chassé). (See note above.)	(2) The Quarter Turns.

Fish Tail

LADY

Begin backing diag. to centre and finish backing diag. to wall.

1. Back L.F., in C.B.M.P., P.O.	⎱ Turning to R.	S.
2. Cross R.F. in front of L.F.	⎰ to back diag.	Q.
3. Short step diag. back L.F.	to wall.	Q.
4. Diag. back R.F.		Q.
5. Cross L.F. in front of R.F.		Q.
6. Diag. back R.F.		S.
7. Back L.F., in C.B.M.P., P.O.		S.

Amount of turn: Make ¼ turn to R. between 1 and 3.
Footwork: 1. T. 2. T. 3. T. 4. T. 5. T. 6. T.H. 7. T.
Contrary body movement: Used on 1 and 7.
Body sway: Sway to L. on 2.

For preceding and following figs. for the Fish Tail, see below the description of gentleman's steps.

Quick Open Reverse Turn

GENTLEMAN

Begin facing L.O.D. and finish according to which figure is to follow
the Quick Open Reverse.

1. Forward L.F.	} Turning to	s.
2. Side R.F.	} L. to back	Q.
3. Back L.F., in C.B.M.P., P.O.	} L.O.D.	Q.
4. Back R.F. (partner in front).		s.

Amount of turn: Make ½ turn to L. between 1 and 3; make ⅜ or ½
turn on 4 if making it a Reverse Pivot.
Footwork: 1. H.T. 2. T. 3. T.H. 4. T.
Contrary body movement: Used on 1 and 4.
Body sway: Sway L. on 2 and 3.

LADY

Begin backing L.O.D. and finish according to which figure is to
follow the Quick Open Reverse.

1. Back R.F.	} Turning to L. to	s.
2. Side L.F., slightly forward.	} face L.O.D.	Q.
3. Forward R.F., O.P., in C.B.M.P.		Q.
4. Forward L.F. (in front of partner).		s.

Amount of turn: Make ½ turn to L. between 1 and 2; make ⅜ or ½
turn on 4 if making it a Reverse Pivot.
Footwork: 1. T.H. 2. T. 3. T.H. 4. H.
Contrary body movement: Used on 1 and 4.
Body sway: Sway to R. on 2 and 3.

This fig. may be preceded by:
(1) Any Heel Pivot.
(2) The Double Reverse Spin.
(3) The Reverse Pivot.
(4) The Progressive Chassé ended
diag. to centre or along
L.O.D.

This fig. may be followed by:
(1) A Reverse Pivot on the fourth
step into the Quick Open
Reverse Turn, any Reverse
Turn, the Zig-Zag, or the
Running Zig-Zag.
(2) The Progressive Chassé when
fourth step will be the first of
Progressive Chassé.
(3) The Heel Pivot.
(4) The Corté, when fourth step
will be first of the Corté.
(5) The Four Quick Run.

Check and Four Quick Run

GENTLEMAN

At a corner, having danced a Progressive Chassé, you will be facing
diag. to wall. Finish the Four Quick Run facing diag. to wall of
"new" L.O.D.

Check	{ 1. Back L.F., in C.B.M.P., P.O.	} Towards the	"new" centre.	s.
	{ 2. Back R.F. (partner in front).			s.
	(3. Side L.F., slightly forward (facing wall).			Q.
Four		4. Forward R.F., O.P., in C.B.M.P. (diag. to wall).		Q.
Quick	< 5. Diag. forward L.F.			Q.
Run		6. Cross R.F. behind L.F.		Q.
	(7. Diag. forward L.F.			s.
	(8. Forward R.F., O.P., in C.B.M.P.			s.

Amount of turn: Make ¼ turn to L. between the last step of the
Progressive Chassé and step 4.

Footwork: 1. T.H. 2. T.H.T. 3. T. 4. T. 5. T. 6. T. 7. T.H.
8. H.

Contrary body movement: Used on 2 and 8.

Body sway: Nil.

These figs. may be preceded by:	*These figs. may be followed by:*
(1) Any Progressive Chassé ended at a corner.	(1) Any Natural fig.
(2) Any fig. ended O.P. on R.F. (lady back L.F., P.O.) (i.e. the Running Zig-Zag or the Running Right Turn).	(2) The Forward Lock Step.
	(3) The Fish Tail.

Note. The Four Quick Run may be danced without the Check, when
it could be preceded by the Quick Open Reverse Turn or the first
four steps of the Chassé Reverse Turn.

Check and Four Quick Run

LADY

At a corner, having danced a Progressive Chassé, you will be backing
diag. to wall. Finish the Four Quick Run backing diag. to wall
of "new" L.O.D.

Check	{1. Forward R.F.} Towards "new" centre.		S.
	{2. Forward L.F.}		S.
	3. Side R.F. (backing to wall).		Q.
Four	4. Back L.F., in C.B.M.P., P.O. (diag. to wall).		Q.
Quick	5. Diag. back R.F.		Q.
Run	6. Cross L.F. in front of R.F.		Q.
	7. Diag. back R.F.		S.
	8. Back L.F., in C.B.M.P., P.O.		S.

Amount of turn: Make ¼ turn to L. between last step of Progressive
Chassé and step 4.
Footwork: 1. H. 2. H.T. 3. T. 4. T. 5. T. 6. T. 7. T.H. 8. T.
Contrary body movement: Used on 2 and 8.
Body sway: Nil.
Note. For preceding and following figs. for the Check and Four
Quick Run see below the description of gentleman's steps.

Running Right Turn

This figure is usually used across a corner as described below.

GENTLEMAN

Begin facing diag. to wall and finish facing new L.O.D.

	1, 2, 3, 4. Do the Natural Pivot Turn.	S.Q.Q.S.
	5. Forward on to R.F., in C.B.M.P. (still turning to R.).	S.
	6. Side L.F. (still turning to R.).	S.
	7. Back R.F., preparing to lead P.O.	S.
	{8. Back L.F., in C.B.M.P., P.O. (turning to R.).	Q.
Running	9. Side R.F., slightly forward.	Q.
Finish	10. Forward L.F., preparing to step O.P.	S.
	11. Forward R.F., O.P., in C.B.M.P.	S.

Amount of turn: Across a corner make ⅜ turn to R. on pivot of
Natural Pivot Turn; make ½ turn to R. between 5 and 7; make
⅜ turn to R. between 8 and 9.
Footwork: 1. H.T. 2. T. 3. T.H. 4. T.H.T. 5. H.T. 6. T.
7. T.H. 8. T. 9. T. 10. T.H. 11. H.
Contrary body movement: Used on 1, 4, 5, 8 and 11.
Body sway: Sway to R. on 2 and 3; sway to R. on 6 and 7; sway
to L. on 9 and 10.

This fig. may be preceded by:
(1) Any fig. finished diag. to wall with R.F. free (lady L.F.).

This fig. may be followed by:
(1) Any Natural Turn commencing on L.O.D.
(2) The Quarter Turns.
(3) The Quick Open Reverse Turn (if Running Finish is ended diag. to new centre).
(4) The Fish Tail.

Running Right Turn

LADY

Begin backing diag. to wall and finish backing "new" L.O.D.

	1, 2, 3, 4. Do the Natural Pivot Turn.	s.q.q.s.
	5. Back on to L.F. (still turning to R.).	s.
Heel	6. Close R.F. to L.F. (turning from L. heel on	
Turn	to R.F.).	s.
	7. Forward L.F., preparing to step O.P.	s.
	8. Forward R.F., O.P., in C.B.M.P.	Q.
Running	9. Side L.F.	Q.
Finish	10. Back R.F.	s.
	11. Back L.F., in C.B.M.P., P.O.	s.

Amount of turn: Across a corner make ⅜ turn to R. on pivot of Natural Pivot Turn; make ½ turn to R. between 5 and 6; make ⅜ turn to R. between 8 and 10.

Footwork: 1. T.H. 2. T. 3. T.H. 4. H.T.H. 5. T.H. 6. H.T. 7. T.H. 8. H.T. 9. T. 10. T.H. 11. T.

Contrary body movement: Used on 1, 4, 5, 8 and 11.

Body sway: Sway to L. on 2 and 3; sway to L. on 6 and 7; sway to R. on 9 and 10.

Note. For preceding and following figs. see below the description of gentleman's steps.

Change of Direction

GENTLEMAN

Begin facing diag. to wall and finish facing diag. to centre.

1. Forward L.F.   s.
2. Diag. forward R.F.   Turning to L. to face   s.
3. Close L.F. to R.F., slightly forward,   diag. to centre.
     without weight (relaxing both knees).   s.
4. Forward L.F., in C.B.M.P.   s.

Amount of turn: Make $\frac{1}{4}$ turn to L. between 1 and 3.

Footwork: 1. H.   2. Inside edge of T.H.   3. Inside edge of T. of L.F.   4. H.

Contrary body movement: Used on 1 and 4.

Body sway: Sway to L. on 3, straightening on 4.

LADY

Begin backing diag. to wall and finish backing diag. to centre.

1. Back R.F.   s.
2. Diag. back L.F.   Turning to L. to back   s.
3. Close R.F. to L.F., slightly back, with-   diag. to centre.
     out weight (relaxing both knees).   s.
4. Back R.F., in C.B.M.P.   s.

Amount of turn: Make $\frac{1}{4}$ turn to L. between 1 and 3.

Footwork: 1. T.H.   2. T., inside edge of T.H.   3. Inside edge of T. of R.F.   4. T.

Contrary body movement: Used on 1 and 4.

Body sway: Sway to R. on 3, straightening on 4.

This fig. may be preceded by: *This fig. may be followed by:*
(1) The Quarter Turns or any   (1) Any Reverse fig.
     Heel Pivot.
(2) The Reverse Pivot Turn.
(3) The Double Reverse Spin.

Double Reverse Spin

Although called the Double Reverse Spin, this does not signify that it must be used twice. It is better to use it only once at a time.

Whilst the gentleman does three steps the lady does four, that is why it is counted "slow, slow, quick, quick".

GENTLEMAN

Begin facing L.O.D. and finish facing diag. to wall.

	1. Forward L.F. ⎰Turning to L. to back	s.
	2. Side R.F. ⎱ diag. to wall.	s.
Toe	⎰3, 4. Close L.F. to R.F. (completing turn on	
Pivot	⎱ R.F.	Q.Q.

Amount of turn: Make ⅜ turn to L. between 1 and 2; make ½ turn to L. between 2 and 3.

Footwork: 1. H.T.   2. T.   3. T., L.F., then T.H. of R.F.

Contrary body movement: Used on 1.

Body sway: Nil.

LADY

Begin backing to L.O.D. and finish backing diag. to wall.

	1. Back R.F. ⎱Turning to L.	s.
Heel	⎰2. Close L.F. to R.F., turning⎰to face L.O.D.	
Turn	⎱ from R. heel on to L.F. ⎰	s.
	3. Side R.F., slightly back.	Q.
	4. Cross L.F. in front of R.F.	Q.

Amount of turn: Make ½ turn to L. between 1 and 2; make ⅜ turn to L. between 2 and 4.

Footwork: 1. T.H.   2. H.T.   3. T.   4. T.H.

Contrary body movement: Used on 1.

Body sway: Nil.

This fig. may be preceded by:
(1) Any Heel Pivot.
(2) The Toe Pivot.
(3) The Reverse Pivot.

This fig. may be followed by.
(1) The Cross Chassé or the Cross Swivel.
(2) The Drag.
(3) The Change of Direction.
(4) The Running Zig-Zag, or any Reverse fig.; if turned to end on L.O.D., more turn than above.

Quick Open Reverse Pivot Turn

Actually there are four steps in this figure, but a fifth step is described to enable readers to understand how this figure is linked to the figures following it.

GENTLEMAN

Begin facing L.O.D. and finish according to which figure is to follow the Reverse Pivot.

1, 2, 3. Do 1, 2 and 3 of the Quick Open Reverse Turn.   s.Q.Q.
4. Back R.F., pivoting to L.   s.
5. Forward L.F.   s. or Q.

Amount of turn: On 4 the amount of pivot should vary from ⅛ to ½ of a turn to L. according to which figure you use after it. Also, 5 will be s. or Q., according to which figure is to follow. If the Drag, make about ¼ of a turn on 4, and 5 will be the first step of the Drag (Q.). If the Double Reverse Spin make about a ⅜ of a turn on 4, and 5 will be the first step of the Double Reverse Spin (s.).

Footwork: 1. H.T.   2. T.   3. T.H.   4. T.H.T.   5. H.
Contrary body movement: Used on 1, 4 and 5.
Body sway: 1, 2 and 3 as in the Quick Open Reverse Turn; no sway on 4 and 5.

LADY

Begin backing L.O.D. and finish according to which figure is to follow the Reverse Pivot.

1, 2, 3. Do 1, 2 and 3 of the Quick Open Reverse Turn   s.Q.Q.
4. Forward L.F., pivoting to L.   s.
5. Back R.F.   s. or Q.

Amount of turn: See notes on gentleman's steps.
Footwork: 1. T.H.   2. T.   3. T.H.   4. H.T.H.
Contrary body movement: Used on 1, 4 and 5.
Body sway: 1, 2 and 3 as in the Quick Open Reverse Turn; no sway on 4 and 5.

This fig. may be preceded by:
(1) Any Heel Pivot or Toe Pivot.
(2) A Reverse Pivot ended along L.O.D.
(3) The Change of Direction.

This fig. may be followed by:
(1) The Drag.
(2) The Cross Chassé.
(3) The Zig-Zag.
(4) The Running Zig-Zag or any Reverse fig.
(5) The Cross Swivel.

The Drag

This figure is not unlike the Cross Chassé. The pattern, however, is slightly different and also the timing.

Begin facing the wall and finish facing diag. to wall when preceded by the Reverse Pivot.

1. Forward on to L.F., in C.B.M.P.⎫ Turning to L. to	Q.
2. Side R.F., slightly back. ⎬ face diag. to wall.	Q.
3. Close L.F. to R.F.	S.
4. Forward R.F., O.P., in C.B.M.P.	S.

Amount of turn: Make ⅛ turn to L. between 1 and 2.
Footwork: 1. H.T. 2. T. 3. T.H. 4. H.
Contrary body movement: Used on 1 and 4.
Body sway: Sway to L. on 2 and 3.

Begin backing to wall and finish backing diag. to wall when preceded by the Reverse Pivot.

1. Back on to R.F., in C.B.M.P.⎫ Turning to back	Q.
2. Side L.F., slightly forward. ⎬ diag. to wall.	Q.
3. Close R.F. to L.F.	S.
4. Back L.F., in C.B.M.P., P.O.	S.

Amount of turn: Make ⅛ turn to L. between 1 and 2.
Footwork: 1. T.H. 2. T. 3. T.H. 4. T.
Contrary body movement: Used on 1 and 4.
Body sway: Sway to R. on 2 and 3.

This fig. may be preceded by:	*This fig. may be followed by:*
(1) The Reverse Pivot after 1, 2 and 3 of the Quick Open Reverse Turn, 4 of the Quarter Turns or 6 of the Natural Spin Turn.	(1) Any Natural fig.
	(2) The Lock Step Forward.
	(3) The Fish Tail.

Impetus Turn

This figure is sometimes used in the Quickstep as a change from the other Natural figures.

The pattern is the same as that used in the Slow Foxtrot, but counted s.s.s.s.

The Impetus Turn is followed by 6, 7 and 8 of the Quarter Turns; the Progressive Chassé; or pivot on the last step into any fig. that follows a Reverse Pivot.

The Open Impetus Turn

The pattern and notes are the same as in the Waltz, but counted s.s.s.

The Open Impetus Turn is followed by the Wing, but counted s.Q.Q. (*Note*. For the description of the Wing see the Waltz, page 53.)

The Closed Telemark

The pattern and notes are the same as in the Slow Foxtrot, but counted s.s.s.s.

The Closed Telemark is usually preceded by the Wing (see Waltz), and followed by the Quarter Turns or any Natural Turn.

The Open Telemark

The pattern and notes are the same as in the Slow Foxtrot, but counted s.s.s.s. (without Feather Finish).

The Open Telemark is usually preceded by the Quarter Turns and followed by the Progressive Chassé, dancing the first step in P.P. (or the Wing—see Waltz).

CHAPTER IX

THE TANGO

SOME GENERAL NOTES

THE Tango in its simple form need never take up a lot of room in the ballroom and it is really a very simple dance for beginners to learn. The music is easy to follow as the beats are very well marked; it is written in 2/4 time (i.e., there are two beats to each bar of music). The tempo is about thirty-two bars to the minute, a good steady tempo for a beginner to tackle. It is helpful to listen to the music and to pick out the beats by clapping them in time with the music before learning the figures.

The Hold for the Tango varies very slightly from the other dances. The lady is held very slightly more towards the right side of the gentleman; his right hand is placed a little further round her, so that his right side, from head to foot, is slightly in advance of his left side; this position is characteristic of the Tango Walk Forward. The lady places her left hand a little higher on the gentleman's right upper arm and slightly more towards the back of his arm. The gentleman's left forearm and the lady's right forearm should be curved inwards a little more towards their bodies.

The Walk Forward is almost the same as that used in everyday life, and each step is of natural length. The foot is placed on the floor on the heel first, and then onto the whole foot. Each step takes up one beat of music and is counted "slow". (*Note.* A step in the Tango timed "quick" takes up half a beat only.) Each walking step should be bold and firm; this is very important.

As a result of the Tango hold, each forward walk with the left foot should be placed slightly across the body, and each forward walk with the right foot in an open position (not across the body). The way to obtain the correct position is: As the left foot moves forward, see that the back of the left knee brushes past the front of the right knee; as the right foot moves forward, see that the front of the right knee brushes past the back of the left knee. At the same time be careful to keep the feet in line, with the body pointing slightly to the left as a result of the right side being in advance. These walking steps, when repeated, will curve slightly to the left.

The Backward Walk should also be as natural as possible. When the step has been taken back, the toes should meet the floor first, then the ball of the foot; the heel should not be in contact with the floor until the other foot is brought back and passes it.

As a result of the Tango hold, each backward walk with the right foot will be placed slightly across the body, and each backward walk with the left foot will be in an open position. As in the Forward walk, the easiest way to obtain the correct position is: As the right foot moves backward, see that the front of the right knee brushes past the back of the left knee. As the left foot moves backward, see that the back of the left knee brushes past the front of the right knee. Naturally the backward walks will also curve to the left if repeated.

The Knees should be more relaxed in the Tango because the steps are taken and the feet moved as in normal walking.

Other Characteristics of the Tango. In all figures that end with the feet closed (i.e., the Rock Turn, the Open Reverse Turn, the Closed Promenade, and the Back Corté), the feet should close, gentleman's right foot slightly behind his left foot, lady's left foot slightly in advance of her right foot, if the close is danced facing partner. In Promenade Position, lady's left foot would close a little back.

At the bottom of page 121 and the top of page 122 will be found a very simple routine for the beginner.

Progressive Side Step

GENTLEMAN

Begin facing diag. to wall.

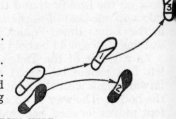

BEGIN HERE

1. Forward L.F.   Q.
2. Side R.F. (almost closed to L.F.) slightly back.   Q.
3. Forward L.F.   S.

Finish facing L.O.D., having curved slightly to L. on 2, or finish facing diag. to wall.

Amount of turn: A slight turn to L. may be made.
Footwork: 1. H. 2. Inside edge of foot. 3. H.
Contrary body movement: Nil (C.B.M.P. on 1 and 3).

Progressive Side Step

LADY

Begin backing diag. to wall.

1. Back R.F.   Q.
2. Side L.F. (almost closed to R.F.) slightly forward.   Q.
3. Back R.F.   S.

Finish backing L.O.D., having curved slightly to L. on 2, or finish backing diag. to wall.

Amount of turn: A slight turn to L. may be made.

Footwork: 1. B.H.   2. Inside edge of B.H.   3. B.

Contrary body movement: Nil (C.B.M.P. on 1 and 3).

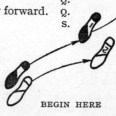

BEGIN HERE

This fig. may be preceded by:	*This fig. may be followed by:*
(1) A walk on R.F. (lady L.F.).	(1) A walk on R.F. (lady L.F.).
(2) The Rock Turn.	(2) The Rock Turn.
(3) The Open Reverse Turn.	
(4) The Closed Promenade.	
(5) The Back Corté.	

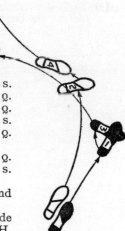

Rock Turn

GENTLEMAN

Begin facing diag. to wall.

1. Forward R.F.   S.
2. Side L.F., slightly back } Make ¼ turn to R.   Q.
3. Forward R.F.   Q.
4. Back L.F.   S.
5. Back R.F.   Q.
6. Side L.F., slightly forward } Make ¼ turn to L.   Q.
7. Close R.F. to L.F.   S.

Finish facing diag. to wall.

Amount of turn: Make ¼ turn to R. between 1 and 3; make ¼ turn to L. between 4 and 6.

Footwork: 1. H.   2. Inside edge of B.H.   3. Inside edge of B.H.   4. Inside edge of B.H.   5. B.H.   6. Inside edge of foot.   7. Whole foot.

Contrary body movement: Used slightly on 1; used on 5 (C.B.M.P. on 5).

BEGIN HERE

Rock Turn

LADY

Begin backing diag. to wall.

1. Back L.F.	s.
2. Forward R.F.	Q.
3. Back L.F.	Q.
4. Forward R.F.	s.
5. Forward L.F.	Q.
6. Side R.F., slightly back.	Q.
7. Close L.F. to R.F.	s.

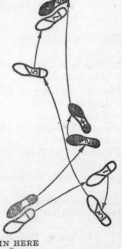

BEGIN HERE

Finish backing diag. to wall.

Amount of turn: Make ¼ turn to R. between 1 and 3; make ¼ turn to L. between 4 and 6.

Footwork: 1. B.H. 2. H. 3. Inside edge of B.H. 4. H. 5. H. 6. Inside edge of B.H. 7. Whole foot.

Contrary body movement: Used slightly on 1; used on 5 (C.B.M.P. on 5).

This fig. may be preceded by:
(1) The Progressive Side Step.
(2) A walk on L.F. (lady R.F.).
(3) The Natural Promenade Turn, making the last step the first of the Rock Turn.

This fig. may be followed by:
(1) A walk on L.F. (lady R.F.).
(2) The Progressive Side Step.
(3) The Back Corté.

Open Reverse Turn

(With partner outside on 3, with closed ending.)

GENTLEMAN

Begin facing diag. to centre.

1. Forward L.F. ⎫
2. Side R.F. ⎬ Turning to L. to   Q.
3. Back L.F., P.O. ⎭ back L.O.D.   Q.
                                     S.
4. Back R.F.   Q.
5. Side L.F., slightly ⎫ Turning to L. to
   forward   ⎬ face diag. to wall. Q.
6. Close R.F. to L.F. ⎭   S.

Finish facing diag. to wall.

Amount of turn: Make ¾ turn to L.
Footwork: 1. H. 2. B.H. 3. B.H. 4. B.H.
   5. Inside edge of foot. 6. Whole foot.
Contrary body movement: Used on 1 and 4
   (C.B.M.P. on 1, 3 and 4).

LADY

Begin backing diag. to centre.

1. Back R.F. ⎫
2. Side L.F. ⎬ Turning to L.   Q.
3. Forward R.F., O.P. ⎭ to face L.O.D. Q.
                                         S.
4. Forward L.F.   ⎫ Turning to L. Q.
5. Side R.F., slightly back ⎬ to back diag. Q.
6. Close L.F. to R.F.   ⎭ to wall.   S.

Finish backing diag. to wall.

Amount of turn: Make ¾ turn to L.
Footwork: 1. B.H. 2. Whole foot, 3. H 4 H.
   5. Inside edge of B.H. 6. Whole foot.
Contrary body movement: Used on 1 and 4
   (C.B.M.P. on 1, 3 and 4).

This fig. may be preceded by:
(1) A walk on R.F. (lady L.F.)

This fig. may be followed by:
(1) A walk on L.F. (lady R.F.).
(2) The Progressive Side Step.
(3) The Back Corté (at a corner).

BEGIN HERE

BEGIN HERE

BEGIN
HERE

Closed Promenade

GENTLEMAN

Begin sideways on to L.O.D., with toes pointing
    diag. to wall (P.P.).
1. Side L.F., in P.P.   s.
2. Forward and across L.F. with R.F., in
    P.P.   Q.
3. Side L.F., slightly forward   Q.
4. Close R.F. to L.F.   s.
Finish facing diag. to wall, with partner
    facing square to you.

Amount of turn: Nil.
Footwork: 1. H. 2. H. 3. Inside edge of
    foot. 4. Whole foot.
Contrary body movement: Nil (C.B.M.P.
    on 2).

LADY

Begin sideways on to L.O.D., with toes pointing
    diag. to centre (P.P.).
1. Side R.F., in P.P.   s.
2. Forward and across R.F. with L.F.,
    in P.P.   Q.
3. Side R.F., slightly back, turning to L.
    to face square to partner.   Q.
4. Close L.F. to R.F.   s.
Finish backing diag. to wall.
Amount of turn: Make ¼ turn to L. between 2 and 3.
Footwork: 1. H. 2. H. 3. Inside edge of B.H.
    4. Whole foot.
  Contrary body movement: On 2, when lady turns
    square to partner (C.B.M.P. on 2).

This fig. may be preceded by:
(1) A walk on R.F., brushing
L.F. towards R.F. before
moving it sideways for 1
of the Closed Promenade
(lady brushing R.F.).
(2) The Natural Promenade
Turn, brushing L.F. to-
wards R.F. before moving
it sideways for 1 of the
Closed Promenade (lady
brushing R.F.).

This fig. may be followed by:
(1) A walk on L.F. (lady R.F.).
(2) The Progressive Side Step.
(3) Another Closed Promenade
if the lady is kept in P.P.
instead of turning square
to partner on 3 of the first
Closed Promenade.
(4) The Back Corté.
(5) The Natural Promenade
Turn if lady is kept in P.P.
throughout the Closed
Promenade (see 3 above).

BEGIN
HERE

Back Corté

GENTLEMAN

Begin backing down L.O.D., or "new" L.O.D. if used
at a corner.

1. Back L.F.   s.
2. Back R.F. ⎫   Q.
3. Side L.F. ⎬ Make ¼ turn to L.   Q.
4. Close R.F. to L.F.   s.

Finish facing diag. to wall (or "new" wall).

Amount of turn: Make up to ¼ turn to L. between 2
and 3.

Footwork: 1. Inside edge of B.H. 2. B.H. 3. Inside
edge of foot. 4. Whole foot.

Contrary body movement: Used on 2 (C.B.M.P. on 2).

BEGIN HERE

LADY

Begin forward down L.O.D., or "new" L.O.D. if used
at a corner.

1. Forward R.F.   s.
2. Forward L.F. ⎫   Q.
3. Side R.F.   ⎬ Make ¼ turn to L.   Q.
4. Close L.F. to R.F.   s.

Finish backing diag. to wall (or "new" wall).

Amount of turn: Make up to ¼ turn to L. between 2 and
3.

Footwork: 1. H. 2. H. 3. Inside edge of B.H. 4. Whole
foot.

Contrary body movement: Used on 2 (C.B.M.P. on 2).

This fig. may be preceded by:
(1) The Rock Turn, used near a
    corner.
(2) The Open Reverse Turn, used
    near a corner.
(3) The Closed Promenade, used
    near a corner.

BEGIN
HERE

(4) Any of the above figures used
    on the sides of the ballroom
    if no turn is made on the
    Back Corté and it is com-
    menced and finished facing
    diag. to wall (lady backing
    diag. to wall).

This fig. may be followed by:
(1) A walk on L.F. (lady R.F.).
(2) The Progressive Side Step.
(3) The Back Corté, repeated if
    no turn is used on it the first
    time it is danced.

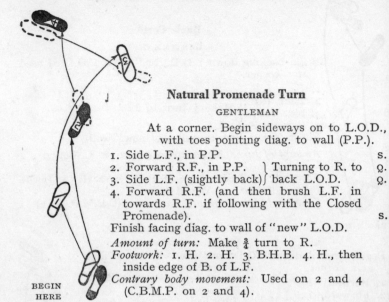

BEGIN
HERE

Natural Promenade Turn

GENTLEMAN

At a corner. Begin sideways on to L.O.D.,
with toes pointing diag. to wall (P.P.).

1. Side L.F., in P.P.   s.
2. Forward R.F., in P.P.   } Turning to R. to   Q.
3. Side L.F. (slightly back) } back L.O.D.   Q.
4. Forward R.F. (and then brush L.F. in
   towards R.F. if following with the Closed
   Promenade).   s.

Finish facing diag. to wall of "new" L.O.D.

Amount of turn: Make ¾ turn to R.

Footwork: 1. H. 2. H. 3. B.H.B. 4. H., then
inside edge of B. of L.F.

Contrary body movement: Used on 2 and 4
(C.B.M.P. on 2 and 4).

Natural Promenade Turn

LADY

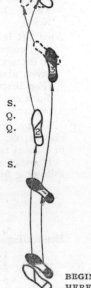

BEGIN
HERE

At a corner. Begin sideways on to L.O.D., with toes pointing diag. to centre (P.P.).

1. Side R.F., in P.P.
2. Forward L.F. and across R.F., in P.P.
3. Forward R.F. (between partner's feet).
4. Side L.F. (and slightly back from R.F.), and then brush R.F. towards L.F. if following with the Closed Promenade.

Finish step 4 = side step with L.F., backing diag. to "new" wall, and continue to turn (as you brush R.F. towards L.F.) into P.P. sideways on to "new" L.O.D., with toes pointing diag. to "new" centre.

Amount of turn: Make ¾ turn to R.
Footwork: 1. H. 2. H. 3. H. 4. B.H., then inside edge of B. of R.F.
Contrary body movement: Used on 3 only (C.B.M.P. on 2).

This fig. may be preceded by:
(1) A walk on R.F. (lady L.F.), opening to P.P. as for the Closed Promenade.
(2) The Closed Promenade, when lady is kept in P.P. and *not* turned square to partner.

This fig. may be followed by:
(1) The Closed Promenade.
(2) The Rock Turn, when the last step of the Promenade Turn will become the first step of the Rock Turn.

Simple Routine for Practising the Tango

(For Gentlemen)

Two walks, L.F., R.F.; Progressive Side Step; Rock Turn; *then*
Two walks, L.F., R.F.; Progressive Side Step; one walk, R.F., Open Reverse Turn; *then*
Two walks, L.F., R.F.; Progressive Side Step; one walk, R.F., opening into P.P.; Closed Promenade (turning partner square); *then*
Two walks, L.F., R.F.; Progressive Side Step; one walk, R.F., opening into P.P.; Natural Promenade Turn if at a corner; Closed Promenade.

To introduce the Back Corté, dance it after any figure in the above sequences which ends with the feet closed (i.e. the Open Reverse Turn, the Closed Promenade (partner square), the Rock Turn). Following the Back Corté, go into the two walks, L.F., R.F.

Note. It is not necessary for ladies to study this routine; it is for gentlemen who have difficulty in making up their minds what to do next. These amalgamations need not be danced in the order given above; it depends largely on where you are in the room. (For instance, the fourth one including the Natural Promenade Turn could be danced first if you were commencing fairly near a corner.)

I have found this routine and variations of it most useful for classes; especially for pupils who wish to learn to tackle the Tango in a short time.

Having mustered the above the pupil can now pass on to the following figures.

Closed Reverse Turn

GENTLEMAN

Begin diag. to centre and finish facing diag. to wall.

	1. Forward L.F., in C.B.M.P.	Q.
	2. Side R.F., slightly back (backing L.O.D.).	Q.
	3. Cross L.F. in front of R.F.	s.
Closed Ending	4. Back R.F.	Q.
	5. Side L.F., slightly forward.	Q.
	6. Close R.F. to L.F., slightly back.	s.

Amount of turn: Make ⅜ turn to L. between 1 and 2; make ⅜ turn to L. between 4 and 6 (or no turn on 4, 5 and 6).

Footwork: 1. H. 2. B.H. 3. Whole foot. 4. B.H. 5. Inside edge of foot. 6. Whole foot.

Contrary body movement: Used on 1 and 4.

This fig. may be preceded by:
(1) A walk on R.F. (lady L.F.).

This fig. may be followed by:
(1) A walk on L.F. (lady R.F.).
(2) Any Promenade fig. if gentleman opens partner to P.P. on the Closed Ending.
(3) The Progressive Side Step.
(4) The Rock (No. 1) or Back Corté at a corner, or if the Closed Ending is danced without any turn.
(5) The Progressive Link.
(6) The Four Step.
(7) The Promenade Link or the Fallaway Promenade, if gentleman opens lady to P.P. on the Closed Ending.

Closed Reverse Turn

LADY

Begin backing diag. to centre and finish in P.P. facing diag. to centre, or square to partner backing diag. to wall.

1. Back R.F. in C.B.M.P.	Q.
2. Side L.F slightly forward.	Q.
3. Close R.F. to L.F., slightly back (facing L.O.D.).	S.

Closed Ending
4. Forward L.F.	Q.
5. Side R.F. slightly back.	Q.
6. Close L.F. to R.F. slightly forward.	S.

Amount of turn: Make ⅜ turn to L. between 1 and 3; make ⅜ turn to L. between 4 and 6 (or no turn on 4, 5 and 6).
Footwork: 1. B.H.   2. Whole foot.   3. Whole foot.   4. H.   5. Inside edge of B.H.   6. Whole foot.
Contrary body movement: Used on 1 and 4.

For preceding and following figs. for the Closed Reverse Turn, see below the description of gentleman's steps.

Open Promenade

This figure is taken sideways to the line of dance.

GENTLEMAN

Begin in P.P., facing diag. to wall, and finish between wall and diag. to wall.

1, 2. Do 1 and 2 of the Closed Promenade.	S.Q.
3. Side L.F., slightly forward (turning partner square).	Q.
4. Forward R.F., O.P., in C.B.M.P.	S.

Amount of turn: Make slight turn to R. between 2 and 3.
Contrary body movement: Nil.

LADY

Begin in P.P., facing diag. to centre and finish backing between wall and diag. to wall.

1, 2. Do 1 and 2 of the Closed Promenade.	S.Q.
3. Side R.F., slightly back (turning square to partner).	Q.
4. Back with L.F., in C.B.M.P., P.O.	S.

Amount of turn: Make nearly ¼ turn to L. between 2 and 3.
Contrary body movement: Used on 2.

This fig. may be preceded by:
(1) A walk on R.F., brushing L.F. to R.F. without weight, opening to P.P.
(2) Any Closed Ending, when lady is opened to P.P.
(3) The Back Corté, opening lady to P.P.
(4) The Natural Twist Turn.
(5) The Natural Promenade Turn, brushing L.F. to R.F. without weight, opening to P.P.
(6) The Progressive Link.
(7) The Four Step.

This fig. may be followed by:
(1) A walk on L.F.
(2) The Progressive Side Step.
(3) The Back Corté, commenced with P.O. on first step.
(4) The Rock (No. 1) and the Closed Ending.
(5) The Progressive Link.
(6) The Four Step.

Open Reverse Turn

(Lady in front on 3)

This figure can be danced in two ways. The most popular way is to do 1, 2 and 3 (described below), and then finish with 4, 5 and 6 of the Closed Reverse Turn = Closed Ending.

The open ending given below may be used as an ending instead of the Closed Ending for any Reverse Turn.

GENTLEMAN

Begin facing diag. to centre and finish facing diag. to wall.

	1. Forward L.F., in C.B.M.P.	Q.
	2. Side R.F., slightly back.	Q.
	3. Back L.F. (down L.O.D.).	S.
Open Ending	4. Back R.F.	Q.
	5. Side L.F., slightly forward.	Q.
	6. Forward R.F., O.P., in C.B.M.P.	S.

Amount of turn: Make just under ¾ turn to L. on this fig.
Footwork: 1. H.   2. B.H.   3. Inside edge of B.H.   4. B.H.   5. Inside edge of foot.   6. H.
Contrary body movement: Used on 1 and 4.

LADY

Begin backing diag. to centre and finish backing diag. to wall.

	1. Back R.F., in C.B.M.P.	Q.
	2. Close L. heel to R. heel.	Q.
	3. Forward R.F. (down L.O.D.).	S.
Open Ending	4. Forward L.F.	Q.
	5. Side R.F., slightly back.	Q.
	6. Back L.F., in C.B.M.P., P.O.	S.

Amount of turn: Make just under ¾ of a turn to L. on this fig.
Contrary body movement: Used on 1 and 4.

This fig. may be preceded by:
(1) A walk on R.F. (lady L.F.).

This fig. may be followed by:
(1) A walk on L.F.
(2) The Progressive Side Step.
(3) The Progressive Link.
(4) The Back Corté, danced with lady outside on 1.
(5) The Four Step.

Natural Twist Turn

GENTLEMAN

Begin and finish in P.P., feet facing diag. to wall, or finish with
  back diag. to centre, when the Back Corté is to follow.

1. Side L.F., in P.P.   S.
2. Forward R.F. and across in P.P. and C.B.M.P.   Q.
3. Side L.F. (backing diag. to centre).   Q.
4. Cross R.F. behind L.F., with feet apart (back to L.O.D.).   S.
5.} Twist just over ⅜ turn to R. (on L. heel and ball of R.F.),
6.} finishing with weight on R.F. (finish with feet almost
    closed together).   Q.Q.

Amount of turn: Make ⅝ of a turn to R. between 2 and 4. (Make
  just over ¾ of a turn on 5 and 6 when the Back Corté is to follow).
Footwork: 1. H. 2. H. 3. B.H. 4. B. 5, 6. Begin on B. of R.F.
  and H. of L.F., end on whole foot R.F. and inside edge of B. of L.F.
Contrary body movement. Used on 2.

LADY

Begin and finish in P.P., feet facing diag. to centre.

1. Side R.F., in P.P.   S.
2. Forward L.F. and across in P.P. and C.B.M.P.   Q.
3. Forward R.F. (between partner's feet, down L.O.D.).   Q.
4. Forward L.F., preparing to step O.P.   S.
5. Forward R.F., O.P., in C.B.M.P. (to wall).   Q.
6. Close L.F. to R.F. (facing diag. to centre).   Q.

Amount of turn: Make a complete turn to R.
Footwork: 1. H. 2. H. 3. H. 4. H. 5. H.B. 6. B.H.
Contrary body movement: Used on 3 and 5.

This fig. may be preceded by:
(1) Any Promenade fig. except the Open Promenade.
(2) A walk on R.F., opening lady to P.P.
(3) Any Closed Finish, opening lady to P.P.
(4) The Progressive Link.
(5) The Four Step.
(6) The Fallaway Promenade.

This fig. may be followed by:
(1) Any Promenade fig.
(2) The Back Corté.
(3) The Rock (No. 1) and the Closed Ending.
(4) The Promenade Link.
(5) The Fallaway Promenade.

Progressive Side Step Reverse Turn

(With Rock [No.1] and Closed Ending)

GENTLEMAN

Begin facing diag. to centre and finish facing diag. to wall.

Progressive Side Step	1. Forward L.F., in C.B.M.P.	Turning to L. about ½ turn.	Q.
	2. Side R.F., slightly back.		S.
	3. Forward L.F., in C.B.M.P.		S.
	4. Forward R.F.		S.
Rock No. 1	5. Back on to L.F.	No turn.	Q.
	6. Forward on to R.F.		Q.
	7. Back L.F., small step.		S.
Closed Ending	8. Back R.F., in C.B.M.P.	Turning to L.	Q.
	9. Side L.F., slightly forward.		Q.
	10. Close R.F. to L.F., slightly back.		S.

Amount of turn: Make ¾ turn to L.
Footwork: 1. H. 2. Inside edge of foot. 3. H. 4. H. 5. Inside edge of B.H. 6. H. 7. Inside edge of B.H. 8. B.H. 9. Inside edge of foot. 10. Whole foot.
Contrary body movement: Used on 1, 3 and 8.

This fig. may be preceded by:
(1) A walk on R.F. (lady L.F.).

This fig. may be followed by:
(1) A walk on L.F. (lady R.F.).
(2) Any Promenade fig. if lady is opened to P.P. on the Closed Ending.
(3) The Progressive Side Step.
(4) The Progressive Link.
(5) The Four Step.

(6) The Promenade Link or Fallaway Promenade if lady is
opened to P.P. on the Closed
Ending.

After the first four
steps of the Pro-
gressive Side Step
Reverse Turn.

(7) (a) The Back Corté.
(b) The Rock (No. 1 and No.
2) into the Back Corté.
(c) The Rock (No. 1). Walk
R.F. back S. and forward
L.F., in C.B.M.P., into a Progressive Side Step, turning to
end diag. to wall.

Progressive Side Step Reverse Turn

LADY

Begin backing diag. to centre and finish backing diag. to wall.

Progressive Side Step	1. Back R.F., in C.B.M.P.		Q.
	2. Side L.F., slightly forward.	Turning to L. about ½ turn.	Q.
	3. Back R.F., in C.B.M.P.		S.
	4. Back L.F.		S.
Rock (No. 1)	5. Forward onto R.F.		Q.
	6. Back onto L.F.	No turn.	Q.
	7. Forward R.F., small step.		S.
Closed Ending	8. Forward L.F., in C.B.M.P.		Q.
	9. Side R.F., slightly back.	Turning to L.	Q.
	10. Close L.F. to R.F., slightly forward.		S.

Amount of turn: Make ¾ turn to L.

Footwork: 1. B.H. 2. Inside edge of foot. 3. B.H. 4. Inside
edge of B.H. 5. H. 6. Inside edge of B.H. 7. H. 8. H.
9. Inside edge of B.H. 10. Whole foot.

Contrary body movement: Used on 1, 3 and 8.

For preceding and following figs. for the Progressive Side Step
Reverse Turn, see below the description of gentleman's steps.

The Rock (No. 1)

GENTLEMAN

Begin and finish down L.O.D., moving backwards.

1. Back L.F. (down L.O.D.).	Q.
2. Rock forward on to R.F. (against L.O.D.).	Q.
3. Back on to L.F., small step (down L.O.D.).	S.

Amount of turn: Nil.
Footwork: 1. Inside edge of B.H.   2. H.   3. Inside edge of B.H.
Contrary body movement: Nil.

LADY

Begin and finish down L.O.D., moving forwards.

1. Forward R.F. (down L.O.D.).	Q.
2. Rock back on to L.F. (against L.O.D.).	Q.
3. Forward on to R.F., small step (down L.O.D.).	S.

This figure is followed by 4, 5 and 6 of the Closed Reverse Turn, or step forward L.F. into the Progressive Side Step (see 8, 9, 10 and 11 on previous page).

Amount of turn: Nil.
Footwork: 1. H.   2. Inside edge of B.H.   3. H.
Contrary body movement: Nil.

This fig. may be preceded by:
(1) Any Closed Ending ended back to L.O.D.
(2) The Open Promenade at a corner, when the Rock will be danced P.O. throughout.
(3) The Rock (No. 2).
(4) 1, 2, 3 and 4 (as part of Progressive Side Step Reverse Turn).
(5) The Natural Twist Turn, when the Rock will be danced diag. to centre.

This fig. may be followed by:
(1) The Rock (No. 2).
(2) The Closed Ending.
(3) The Open Ending.

The Rock (No. 2)

GENTLEMAN

Begin and finish down L.O.D., moving backwards.

1. Back R.F., in C.B.M.P. (down L.O.D.).   Q.
2. Rock forward on to L.F., in C.M.B.P. (against L.O.D.).   Q.
3. Rock back on to R.F., small step, in C.B.M.P. (down
   L.O.D.).   S.

Amount of turn: Nil.
Footwork: 1. B.H. 2. H. 3. B.H.
Contrary body movement: Nil.

LADY

Begin and finish down L.O.D., moving forward.

1. Forward L.F., in C.B.M.P. (down L.O.D.).   Q.
2. Rock back on to R.F., in C.B.M.P. (against L.O.D.).   Q.
3. Forward on to L.F., small step, in C.B.M.P. (down
   L.O.D.).   S.

Amount of turn: Nil.
Footwork: 1. H. 2. B.H. 3. H.
Contrary body movement: Nil.

This fig. may be preceded by:	*This fig. may be followed by:*
(1) The Rock (No. 1).	(1) The Back Corté.
(2) The first step of Back Corté.	(2) The Rock (No. 1).

Progressive Link

GENTLEMAN

Begin diag. to wall and finish in P.P. diag. to wall.

1. Forward L.F., in C.B.M.P.   Q.
2. Side R.F., slightly back in P.P.   Q.

Amount of turn: The body turns slightly to R. on 2.
Footwork: 1. H. 2. Inside edge of foot and inside edge of B. of L.F.
Contrary body movement: Nil.

LADY

Begin backing diag. to wall and finish in P.P. facing diag. to centre.

1. Back R.F., in C.B.M.P.   Q.
2. Side L.F., slightly back, in P.P.   Q.

Amount of turn: Make ¼ turn to R. between 1 and 2.
Footwork: 1. B.H. 2. Inside edge of B.H. and inside edge of
   B. of R.F.
Contrary body movement: Nil.

E

This fig. may be preceded by:
(1) A walk on R.F. (lady L.F.).
(2) Any Closed Ending.
(3) The Back Corté.
(4) The Open Promenade.
(5) The Open Ending.
(6) The Promenade Link.

This fig. may be followed by:
(1) Any fig, commenced in P.P. (i.e. the Natural Twist Turn, the Natural Promenade Turn, or the Promenades, etc.).

Promenade Link

GENTLEMAN

Begin in P.P. and finish facing the wall.

1. Side L.F., in P.P.   S.
2. Forward R.F. and across in P.P. and C.B.M.P.   Q.
3. Close L.F. to R.F., keeping weight on R.F., turning slightly to R. (to face wall).   Q.

Amount of turn: Make ⅛ turn to R. on 3.
Footwork: 1. H.   2. H.B. (foot flat).   3. Inside edge of B.
Contrary body movement: Used on 2.

LADY

Begin in P.P. and finish backing wall.

1. Side R.F., in P.P.   S.
2. Forward L.F. and across in P.P. and C.B.M.P.   Q.
3. Close R.F. to L.F., keeping weight on L.F., turning slightly to L. (to back to wall).   Q.

Amount of turn: Make ⅛ turn to L. on 3.
Footwork: 1. H.   2. H.B. (foot flat).   3. Inside edge of B.
Contrary body movement: Used on 2.

This fig. may be preceded by:
(1) A walk on R.F. (lady L.F.).
(2) Any Closed Finish danced opening lady to P.P.
(3) The Back Corté, danced opening lady to P.P.
(4) The Natural Twist Turn.
(5) The Natural Promenade Turn danced brushing L.F. in to R.F. after Promenade Turn and opening lady to P.P.
(6) The Progressive Link.
(7) The Four Step.
(8) The Fallaway Promenade.

This fig. may be followed by:
(1) The Progressive Side Step.
(2) The Progressive Link.
(3) The Four Step.
(4) The Walk on L.F. (lady R.F.).
(5) The Promenade Link, danced with man and lady turning to L., when it will be commenced facing L.O.D. and travel diag. to centre. To follow, dance any Reverse fig.

Four Step

GENTLEMAN

Begin facing the wall and finish in P.P. facing diag. to wall.

1. Forward L.F. in C.B.M.P.   Q.
2. Side R.F., slightly back.   Q.
3. Back L.F., in C.B.M.P., P.O.   Q.
4. Close R.F. to L.F., slightly back in P.P.   Q.

Amount of turn: Make ⅛ turn to L. between 1 and 2, or no turn.
Footwork: 1. H. 2. B.H. 3. B.H. 4. B.H.
Contrary body movement: Used on 1.

LADY

Begin with back to wall and finish in P.P. facing diag. to centre.

1. Back R.F., in C.B.M.P.   Q.
2. Side L.F., slightly forward.   Q.
3. Forward R.F., in C.B.M.P., O.P.   Q.
4. Close L.F. to R.F., slightly back, in P.P.   Q.

Amount of turn: Make ⅛ turn to L. between 1 and 2; make ¼ turn to R. between 3 and 4.
Footwork: 1. B.H. 2. Whole foot. 3. H.B. (foot flat). 4. B.H.

This fig. may be preceded by:	*This fig. may be followed by:*
(1) Any Closed Ending.	(1) Any Promenade fig. (i.e. the
(2) The Back Corté.	Natural Twist Turn, the
(3) The Open Promenade.	Natural Promenade Turn,
(4) The Open Ending.	the Fallaway Promenade, the
(5) The Promenade Link.	Closed or Open Promenade.

Fall Away Promenade

GENTLEMAN

Begin in P.P. along L.O.D. and finish in P.P. facing wall.

1. Side L.F., in P.P.   S.
2. Forward R.F. and across in P.P. and C.B.M.P.   Q.
3. Side L.F., still in P.P. (backing almost diag. to centre).   Q.
4. Back R.F., in F.A.P. (to centre, backing diag. to centre).   S.
5. Back L.F., in F.A.P. and C.B.M.P.   Q.
6. Close R.F. to L.F., slightly back, in P.P.   Q.

Amount of turn: Make ¼ turn to R. between 1 and 4; make ⅛ turn to L. between 4 and 5.
Footwork: 1. H. 2. H. 3. B.H. 4. Inside edge of B.H. 5. B.H. 6. B.H.
Contrary body movement: Used on 2.

Fall Away Promenade

LADY

Begin in P.P. along L.O.D. and finish in P.P. facing L.O.D.

1. Side R.F., in P.P.   s.
2. Forward L.F. and across in P.P. and C.B.M.P.   Q.
3. Forward R.F., in P.P. and C.B.M.P.   Q.
4. Back L.F., in F.A.P.   s.
5. Back R.F., in F.A.P. and C.B.M.P.   Q.
6. Close L.F. to R.F., slightly back in P.P.   Q.

Amount of turn: Make ¼ turn to R. between 1 and 4; make ⅛ turn to L. between 5 and 6.

Footwork: 1. H.   2. H.   3. H.   4. Inside edge of B.H.   5. B.H.
6. Whole foot.

Contrary body movement: Used on 3 and 5.

This fig. may be preceded by:	*This fig. may be followed by:*
(1) A walk on R.F. (lady L.F.), lady opened to P.P.	(1) Any Promenade fig. danced diag. to wall (i.e. the Natural Twist Turn, or the Natural Promenade Turn).
(2) The Four Step.	
(3) The Progressive Link.	
(4) The Natural Twist Turn.	

CHAPTER X

THE RUMBA

SOME GENERAL NOTES

THE Rumba has a fascinating rhythm. The figures in their simple form are not difficult to learn, but the hip-movement is not easy and a beginner should not worry about it until the patterns of the figures have been mastered. Rumba music is written in 4/4 time, played at about forty bars per minute.

To understand the rhythm of this dance, it is necessary to divide each bar of music into eight parts (quavers) or half-beats as follows—1,2,3 4,5,6 7,8 half-beats = 1 bar.

When playing this rhythm, most bands accentuate the first, fourth and seventh half-beats, the strongest accent being on the fourth. It is on these strong half-beats that we "step" in Rumba and, although an expert Rumba dancer counts 1,2,3 ($=\frac{3}{8}$ of a bar), 4,5,6 ($=\frac{3}{8}$ of a bar), 7,8 ($=\frac{2}{8}$ of a bar), it is possible to count Rumba music in three counts as follows: 3,1,2—the count 3 $=\frac{3}{8}$ of a bar; the count 1 $=\frac{3}{8}$ of a bar; the count 2 $=\frac{2}{8}$ of a bar.

As in the 8 count (8 quavers), the steps are taken on 1, 4 and 7 and in the music the first and fourth quavers are accentuated, the fourth much more than the first. All figures should begin on this fourth quaver beat, which for convenience is called 1. However, when one starts to dance the Rumba, this would mean that one would have to start with a side step when dancing the squares. To make the first step coincide with the first beat of the bar (instead of the fourth quaver beat) one starts with a forward step to the count 3, followed by a side step counting 1 (accenting this step), and close 2.

For those who find both the "8 count" and the "3 count" difficult, a count of "slow, slow, quick" may be used, although technically the "quick" has not the value of half a "slow", as it has in other dances (i.e.: first "slow" $=\frac{3}{8}$ of the bar; second "slow" $=\frac{3}{8}$ of the bar; and "quick" $=\frac{2}{8}$ of the bar).

The Hold is the same as for the Samba (page 142).

The Hip-movement is obtained by taking the steps with the knee slightly bent, and straightening the knee as the weight is taken onto the foot at the end of the steps.

The body is held erect with the shoulders relaxed; the weight of the body is kept forward toward the balls of the feet; all the steps are danced on the ball of the foot first and then onto the flat foot.

Pupils may feel self-conscious when first dancing these Latin dances, but if they dance without the hip-movement to start with, inhibitions will disappear as confidence gradually grows.

Reverse Left Square (Left)

GENTLEMAN

This fig. is given first as it is more popular than the Natural Right Square as a lead into the other figs.

Danced without turning, or gradually turning to L., repeating the six steps three or four times to make a complete turn to L.

1. Forward L.F.	3 or	S.
2. Side R.F.	1 ,,	S.
3. Close L.F. to R.F.	2 ,,	Q.
4. Back R.F.	3 ,,	S.
5. Side L.F.	1 ,,	S.
6. Close R.F. to L.F.	2 ,,	Q.

LADY

1. Back R.F.	3 or	S.
2. Side L.F.	1 ,,	S.
3. Close R.F. to L.F.	2 ,,	Q.
4. Forward L.F.	3 ,,	S.
5. Side R.F.	1 ,,	S.
6. Close L.F. to R.F.	2 ,,	Q.

Repeat these six steps three or four times to complete a full turn to L.

This fig. may be preceded by:

(1) 1, 2 and 3 of the Natural Square.
(2) The Reverse Top.
(3) The Natural Top, ended with 5 and 6 of the Reverse Square.
(4) The Progressive Walk, ended back R.F. on count 3 into the Reverse Square, beginning with steps 5 and 6.

This fig. may be followed by:

(1) The Reverse Top, after 1, 2, 3 and 4 of the Reverse Square.
(2) The Natural Top after 1 of the Reverse Square.
(3) The Natural Square, after 1, 2 and 3 of the Reverse Square.

Natural Square (Right)

GENTLEMAN

1. Forward R.F.	3 or	S.
2. Side L.F.	1 ,,	S.
3. Close R.F. to L.F.	2 ,,	Q.
4. Back L.F.	3 ,,	S.
5. Side R.F.	1 ,,	S.
6. Close L.F. to R.F.	2 ,,	Q.

Repeat these six steps three or four times if you are turning to R. for a complete turn, or dance the Natural Square with no turn.

LADY

1. Back L.F.	3 or	S.
2. Side R.F.	1 ,,	S.
3. Close L.F. to R.F.	2 ,,	Q.
4. Forward R.F.	3 ,,	S.
5. Side L.F.	1 ,,	S.
6. Close R.F. to L.F.	2 ,,	Q.

To make a complete turn to R. repeat these six steps three or four times.

This fig. may be preceded by:
(1) 1, 2 and 3 of the Reverse Square.

This fig. may be followed by:
(1) 1, 2 and 3 of the Natural Square into the Reverse Square.
(2) 1, 2 and 3 of the Natural Square, then forward with L.F. on count 3 and into a Natural Top.

Progressive Walk

GENTLEMAN

1. Back L.F.		1 or	S.
2. Back R.F.		2 ,,	Q.
3. Back L.F.	These steps	3 ,,	S.
4. Back R.F.	may be curved to L.	1 ,,	S.
5. Back L.F.		2 ,,	Q.
6. Back R.F.		3 ,,	S.

LADY

1. Forward R.F.		1 or	S.
2. Forward L.F.		2 ,,	Q.
3. Forward R.F.	These steps	3 ,,	S.
4. Forward L.F.	may be curved to L.	1 ,,	S.
5. Forward R.F.		2 ,,	Q.
6. Forward L.F.		3 ,,	S.

This fig. may be preceded by:
(1) The first four steps of the Reverse Square.

This fig. may be followed by:
(1) The Reverse Top.
(2) The Reverse Square commenced on the fifth step (side on the count 1).

Side Step

GENTLEMAN

Begin facing the wall (and finish facing wall).

1. Side L.F.	1 or	S.
2. Close R.F. to L.F.	2 ,,	Q.
3. Side L.F.	3 ,,	S.
4. Close R.F. to L.F.	1 ,,	S.
5. Side L.F.	2 ,,	Q.
6. Close R.F. to L.F.	3 ,,	S.
7. Side L.F.	1 ,,	S.
8. Close R.F. to L.F.	2 ,,	Q.

LADY

1. Side R.F.	1 or	S.
2. Close L.F. to R.F.	2 ,,	Q.
3. Side R.F.	3 ,,	S.
4. Close L.F. to R.F.	1 ,,	S.
5. Side R.F.	2 ,,	Q.
6. Close L.F. to R.F.	3 ,,	S.
7. Side R.F.	1 ,,	S.
8. Close L.F. to R.F.	2 ,,	Q.

This fig. may be preceded by:
(1) 1, 2, 3 and 4 of the Reverse Square, turned to face the wall.

This fig. may be followed by:
(1) The Reverse Square.
(2) The Side Step (repeated).

Reverse Top

GENTLEMAN

1. Cross L.F. behind R.F.		1 or s.
2. Side R.F.		2 ,, Q.
3. Cross L.F. behind R.F.	Turning to L.	3 ,, s.
4. Side R.F.	throughout	1 ,, s.
5. Cross L.F. behind R.F.	making about two	2 ,, Q.
6. Side R.F.	complete turns.	3 ,, s.
7. Cross L.F. behind R.F.		1 ,, s.
8. Side R.F.		2 ,, Q.

LADY

1. Side R.F., slightly forward	1 or s.
2. Cross L.F. in front of R.F.	2 ,, Q.
3. Side R.F., slightly forward.	3 ,, s.
4. Cross L.F. in front of R.F.	1 ,, s.
5. Side R.F., slightly forward.	2 ,, Q.
6. Cross L.F. in front of R.F.	3 ,, s.
7. Side R.F.	1 ,, s.
8. Cross L.F. in front of R.F.	2 ,, Q.

This fig. may be preceded by:
(1) 1, 2, 3 and 4 of the Reverse Square.
(2) The Progressive Walk.

This fig. may be followed by:
(1) The Reverse Square.
(2) Forward L.F. (lady back R.F.) on count 3 into Natural Top.

Note. In order to keep facing each other the lady and gentleman must turn the toe *out* on all the "cross" steps, and the toe *in* on all the "side" steps, for the Reverse or the Natural Top, and rotate on an imaginary circle. The hip movement does not occur in these figs.

Natural Top

GENTLEMAN

1. Cross R.F. behind L.F.	1 or s.
2. Side L.F.	2 ,, Q.
3. Cross R.F. behind L.F.	3 ,, s.
4. Side L.F.	1 ,, s.
5. Cross R.F. behind L.F.	2 ,, Q.
6. Side L.F.	3 ,, s.
7. Cross R.F. behind L.F.	1 ,, s.

8. Side L.F.   2 ,, Q.
9. Cross R.F. behind L.F. (or close R.F. to
   L.F.)   3 ,, S.

LADY

1. Side L.F., slightly forward.   1 or S.
2. Cross R.F. in front of L.F.   2 ,, Q.
3. Side L.F., slightly forward.   3 ,, S.
4. Cross R.F. in front of L.F.   1 ,, S.
5. Side L.F., slightly forward.   2 ,, Q.
6. Cross R.F. in front of L.F.   3 ,, S.
7. Side L.F., slightly forward.   1 ,, S.
8. Cross R.F. in front of L.F.   2 ,, Q.
9. Side L.F., slightly forward.   3 ,, S.

This fig. may be preceded by: *This fig. may be followed by:*
(1) The Reverse Square and a   (1) 5 and 6 of the Reverse Square
    step forward with L.F. (lady   into Reverse Square.
    back R.F. on count 3).   (2) Forward on 9 into the Natural
(2) The Reverse Top and a step   Square (lady back).
    forward (as above).

Cuban Walk

GENTLEMAN

1. Side L.F., with half weight on it.   1 or S.
2. Close L.F. to R.F., without weight.   2 ,, Q.
3. Back L.F., transferring weight onto it.   3 ,, S.
4. Side R.F., with half weight on it.   1 ,, S.
5. Close R.F. to L.F., without weight.   2 ,, Q.
6. Back R.F., transferring weight onto it.   3 ,, S.
Repeat these six steps two or three times.

LADY

Dances normal opposite movements.

Note. Before the moving foot is taken to the side, it is brushed close to the stationary foot. This is done to avoid an ugly movement from the foot position preceding the side step.

This fig. may be preceded by: *This fig. may be followed by:*
(1) 1, 2, 3 and 4 of the Reverse   (1) Repeat 1 and 2 of the Cuban
    Square.   Walk, then step forward with
                                         L.F. (lady back R.F.) into the
                                         Reverse Square.

Opening Out from The Reverse Top

GENTLEMAN

1. Side R.F., releasing hold of partner, leading her forward to L. side with the R. hand (retain hold of lady's R. hand in L. hand). 1 or s.
2. Cross L.F. behind R.F. (partner on L. side). 2 ,, Q.
3. Side R.F., slightly forward (partner parallel on L. side). 3 ,, S.
4. Forward and across body with L.F. (knee relaxed), leading partner forward. 1 ,, S.
5. Replace weight onto R.F. 2 ,, Q.
6. Close L.F. to R.F. (partner facing). 3 ,, S.
7, 8, 9. Mark time—R.F., L.F., R.F.—L. arm raised for partner to turn a whole turn to R. (under L. arm). 1 ,, S. 2 ,, Q. 3 ,, S.

This fig. may be preceded by:
(1) The Reverse Top and one extra cross L.F. behind R.F. (9 steps) (lady one extra side step with R.F.).

This fig. may be followed by:
(1) 5 and 6 of the Reverse Square into Reverse Square, when 7, 8 and 9 are danced (the Under Arm).
(2) A Natural Top (if only 1 to 6 are danced).

LADY

1. Forward L.F., turning to L. on partner's L. side. 1 or s.
2. Turning ¼ turn to L., step to side R.F. 2 ,, Q.
3. Turning ¼ turn to L., step back L.F. (short step), relax R. knee, and parallel with partner. 3 ,, s.
4, 5, 6. Progressive walk forward, curving to R. to face partner—R.F., L.F., R.F. 1 ,, s. 2 ,, Q. 3 ,, s.
7, 8, 9. Turning to R. under gentleman's L. arm, steps on the spot—L.F., R.F., L.F. 1 ,, s. 2 ,, Q. 3 ,, s.

For preceding and following figs. see below the description of gentleman's steps.

Opening Out from Natural Top

GENTLEMAN

1. Diag. back R.F., releasing lady's R. hand, turning her } 1 or s.
   to R. into Fallaway.
2. Back L.F., short step in Fallaway (relax R. knee).   2 „ Q.
3. Replace weight onto R.F.   3 „ s.
4. Side L.F., turning partner square.   1 „ s.
5. Close R.F. to L.F.   2 „ Q.

LADY

1. Diag. forward L.F. turning ¼ turn to R.   1 or s.
2. Turning ¼ turn to R., short step back R.F. (relax L. }
   knee), parallel to partner.   2 „ Q.
3. Replace weight onto L.F.   3 „ s.
4. Turning ½ turn to L., side R.F., square to partner.   1 „ s.
5. Close L.F. to R.F.   2 „ Q.

This fig. may be preceded by: *This fig. may be followed by:*
(1) Six steps of Natural Top.   (1) Reverse Square.

American Break

GENTLEMAN

1, 2, 3, 4. Do 1, 2, 3 and 4 of Reverse Square.
5. Side L.F., leading partner to L. with R. hand (release } 1 or s.
   hold, only holding with L. hand).
6. Close R.F. to L.F.   2 „ Q.
7. Forward L.F., partner parallel on L. side.   3 „ s.
8. Side R.F., lead partner forward with L. hand.   1 „ s.
9. Close L.F. to R.F.   2 „ Q.
10. Back R.F.   3 „ s.
11, 12, 13. Progressive Walk backward, curving to R.— } 1 „ s.
   L.F., R.F., L.F. Regain normal hold at end of Pro- } 2 „ Q.
   gressive Walk.   } 3 „ s.

LADY

1, 2, 3, 4. Do 1, 2, 3 and 4 of Reverse Square.
5. Side R.F., turning to L. (partner releases hold).   1 or s.
6. Back L.F., turning to L.   2 „ Q.
7. Back R.F., short step, turning to L., parallel with gen- } 3 „ s.
   tleman on his L. side.

8, 9, 10, 11, 12, 13. Progressive Walk forward, curving to R.—L.F., R.F., L.F., R.F., L.F., R.F. Partner regaining normal hold at the end of these steps.

1	,,	s.
2	,,	Q.
3	,,	s.
1	,,	s.
2	,,	Q.
3	,,	s.

This fig. may be preceded by:
(1) 1, 2, 3 and 4 of the Reverse Square.

This fig. may be followed by:
(1) The Natural Top.
(2) Six steps of the Natural Top into the opening out from the Natural Top.
(3) The Progressive Walk—R.F., L.F., R.F. (lady—L.F., R.F., L.F.)—continuing into 5 and 6 of the Reverse Square or the Reverse Top.

Chapter XI

THE SAMBA

Some General Notes

THE Samba is a lively dance in which there are figures to suit all grades of dancers. The music may be written in 4/4 time, but is more usually written in 2/4 (i.e. two beats to each bar). The tempo is between forty-five and sixty-five bars to the minute. There are four basic rhythms used: (1) s.s. (2) s. and s. (3) s.ǫ.ǫ. (4) ǫ.ǫ.ǫ.ǫ. Most of the figures are really quite simple to learn, but changes from one rhythm to the next require practice.

The Hold. The gentleman's left arm is held higher than in Slow Rhythm, Quick Rhythm and Waltz; it should be about on a level with the top of his left ear. Some of the figures are danced with the gentleman and lady about six inches apart, others close to partner. When the Samba is danced in a crowded ballroom, all the figures should be danced close to partner. The lady may place her left hand higher on the gentleman's right arm than in the other dances.

The Basic Movements of the Samba are danced with a slight bouncing action, obtained by taking each step with the knee relaxed and straightening it slightly as the weight is taken onto the foot. Each forward step should be taken onto the ball or flat of the foot, though it may be taken onto the heel if preferred. I have found that most pupils find it a good idea to think of the bounce as a slight downward springy movement.

In the following pages the figures chosen may be danced either in a spacious ballroom or in a crowded room by using the close hold all the time and very small steps.

Leading the figures in the Samba may present difficulty at first, but if the gentleman remembers that it is quite permissible, and indeed necessary, to lead by using both arms, and the lady keeps her arm-muscles fairly taut to receive his lead, the gentleman will have no difficulty in indicating to his partner which figure he intends to dance.

Natural Right Basic

GENTLEMAN

1. Forward R.F.   S.
2. Close L.F. to R.F., keeping weight on R.F.   S.
3. Back L.F.   S.
4. Close R.F. to L.F., keeping weight on L.F.   S.

Repeat these four steps, turning gradually to R. or making no turn at all (make a complete turn or less, as desired).

LADY

1. Back L.F.   S.
2. Close R.F. to L.F., keeping weight on L.F.   S.
3. Forward R.F.   S.
4. Close L.F. to R.F., keeping weight on R.F.   S.

Repeat these four steps, turning gradually to R. or making no turn at all (make a complete turn or less, as desired).

This fig. may be preceded by:
(1) The Quarter Turns (Progressive Movement).
(2) The Natural Roll.
(3) The Samba Whisk (to L.).
(4) The first two steps of the Reverse Basic (the change from Reverse Left Basic to Natural Basic).
(5) The Outside Movement.

This fig. may be followed by:
(1) The Quarter Turns (Progressive Movement).
(2) The Natural Roll.
(3) The Samba Whisk (to R.).
(4) The Corta Jaca.
(5) The Reverse Left Basic after the first two steps of the Natural Right Basic (the change from Natural Basic to Reverse Basic).

Note.

The change from Natural Basic to Reverse Left Basic—GENTLEMAN:
1. Forward R.F.   S.
2. Close L.F. to R.F., keeping weight on R.F.   S.

The change from Natural Right Basic to Reverse Left Basic—LADY:
1. Back L.F.   S.
2. Close R.F. to L.F., keeping weight on L.F.   S.

Reverse Left Basic

GENTLEMAN

1. Forward L.F.   s.
2. Close R.F. to L.F., keeping weight on L.F.   s.
3. Back R.F.   s.
4. Close L.F. to R.F., keeping weight on R.F.   s.

Repeat these four steps, turning gradually to L. (make a complete
turn or less, as desired).

LADY

1. Back R.F.   s.
2. Close L.F. to R.F., keeping weight on R.F.   s.
3. Forward L.F.   s.
4. Close R.F. to L.F., keeping weight on L.F.   s.

Repeat these four steps, turning gradually to L. (make a complete
turn or less, as desired).

This fig. may be preceded by: *This fig. may be followed by:*
(1) The Reverse Roll.   (1) The Reverse Roll.
(2) The Samba Whisk (to R.).   (2) The Samba Whisk (to L.).
(3) The first two steps of the   (3) The first two steps of the Re-
    Natural Right Basic (the   verse Left Basic (the change
    change from Natural Right   from Reverse Left Basic to
    Basic to Reverse Left Basic).   Natural Right Basic).

Note.
The change from Reverse Left Basic to Natural Right Basic—
GENTLEMAN :

1. Forward L.F.   s.
2. Close R.F. to L.F., keeping weight on L.F.   s.

The change from Reverse Left Basic to Natural Right Basic—LADY :

1. Back R.F.   s.
2. Close L.F. to R.F., keeping weight on R.F.   s.

Quarter Turns or Progressive Movement

GENTLEMAN

Begin facing diag. to wall.
1. Forward R.F.   } ¼ turn   s.
2. Close L.F. to R.F., keeping weight on R.F. } to R.   s.
3. Back L.F.   s.
4. Close R.F. to L.F., keeping weight on L.F.   s.
5. Back R.F.   } ¼ turn   s.
6. Close L.F. to R.F., keeping weight on R.F. } to L.   s.

7. Forward L.F.   s.
8. Close R.F. to L.F., keeping weight on L.   s.
Finish facing diag. to wall.

LADY

Begin backing diag. to wall.

1. Back L.F.   } ¼ turn   s.
2. Close R.F. to L.F., keeping weight on L.F.   } to R.   s.
3. Forward R.F.   s.
4. Close L.F. to R.F., keeping weight on R.F.   s.
5. Forward L.F.   } ¼ turn   s.
6. Close R.F. to L.F., keeping weight on L.F.   } to L.   s.
7. Back R.F.   s.
8. Close L.F. to R.F., keeping weight on R.F.   s.
Finish backing diag. to wall.

This fig. may be preceded by:	*This fig. may be followed by:*
(1) The Natural Basic.	(1) The Natural Basic.
(2) The Quarter Turns (Progressive Movement).	(2) The Natural Roll.
(3) The Natural Roll.	(3) The Quarter Turns (Progressive Movement).
(4) The Samba Whisk (to L.).	(4) The Samba Whisk (to R.).
(5) The Outside Movement.	(5) The Corta Jaca.
	(6) The Outside Movement.

Outside Movement

GENTLEMAN

Begin facing the wall.

1. Forward R.F.   } Make ⅛ turn   s.
2. Close L.F. to R.F., keeping weight on R.F.   } to L. to face
                                                      } diag. to wall. s.
3. Back L.F., P.O.   s.
4. Close R.F. to L.F., keeping weight on L.F.   s.
5. Forward R.F., O.P.   } Make ⅛ turn to s.
6. Close L.F. to R.F., keeping weight on R.F.   } R. to face wall. s.
7. Back L.F.   s.
8. Close R.F. to L.F., keeping weight on L.F.   s.
Finish facing the wall.

LADY

Begin backing the wall.

1. Back L.F.   } Make ⅛ turn   s.
2. Close R.F. to L.F., keeping weight on L.F.   } to L. to back
                                                      } diag. to wall. s.

3. Forward R.F., O.P.   s.
4. Close L.F. to R.F., keeping weight on R.F.   s.
5. Back L.F., P.O.   ⎫ Make ⅛ turn to   s.
6. Close R.F. to L.F., keeping weight on L.F. ⎬ R. to back wall s.
7. Forward R.F.   s.
8. Close L.F. to R.F., keeping weight on R.F.   s.
Finish backing the wall.

This fig. may be preceded by:

(1) The Natural Right Basic, turned to face wall.
(2) The Quarter Turns (Progressive Movement).
(3) The Outside Movement.

This fig. may be followed by:

(1) The Quarter Turns (Progressive Movement).

NOTE. To go into Quarter Turns from the Outside Movement dance 1, 2, 3 and 4 of the Outside Movement, then—forward, R.F. out, O.P., into the Quarter Turns, gentleman turning square to partner on 2 of the Quarter Turns and continuing with 3, 4, 5, 6, 7 and 8 as previously described.

(2) The Natural Right Basic.

Natural Roll

GENTLEMAN

This fig. is danced close to partner (close hold).

1. Forward R.F., leaning back from the waist.   s.
2. Side L.F., leaning to R.   Q.
3. Close R.F. to L.F., leaning slightly forward and to R.   Q.
4. Back L.F., leaning forward from the waist.   s.
5. Side R.F., leaning to L.   Q.
6. Close L.F. to R.F., leaning slightly back and to L.   Q.

Repeat these six steps two or three times, turning gradually to R. until a complete turn (or less) is made.

LADY

This fig. is danced close to partner (close hold).

1. Back L.F., leaning forward from the waist.   s.
2. Side R.F., leaning to L.   Q.
3. Close L.F. to R.F., leaning slightly back and to L.   Q.
4. Forward R.F., leaning back from the waist.   s.
5. Side L.F., leaning to R.   Q.
6. Close R.F. to L.F., leaning slightly forward and to R.   Q.

This fig. may be preceded by:
(1) The Natural Right Basic (bringing lady into a close hold).
(2) The Quarter Turns (Progressive Movement).
(3) The first three steps of the Reverse Roll.
(4) The Corta Jaca followed by 3 and 4 of Natural Right Basic.

This fig. may be followed by:
(1) The Natural Right Basic.
(2) The Quarter Turns (Progressive Movement).
(3) The Corta Jaca.

Reverse Roll

GENTLEMAN

This fig. is danced with a close hold.

1. Forward L.F., leaning back from the waist.   S.
2. Side R.F., leaning to L.   Q.
3. Close L.F. to R.F., leaning slightly forward and to L.   Q.
4. Back R.F., leaning forward from the waist.   S.
5. Side L.F., leaning to R.   Q.
6. Close R.F. to L.F., leaning slightly back and to R.   Q.

Repeat these six steps two or three times, turning gradually to L. until a complete turn (or less) is made.

LADY

This fig. is danced with a close hold.

1. Back R.F., leaning forward from the waist.   S.
2. Side L.F., leaning to R.   Q.
3. Close R.F. to L.F., leaning slightly back and to R.   Q.
4. Forward L.F., leaning back from the waist.   S.
5. Side R.F., leaning to L.   Q.
6. Close L.F. to R.F., leaning slightly forward and to L.   Q.

Repeat these six steps two or three times, turning gradually to L. until a complete turn (or less) is made.

This fig. may be preceded by:
(1) The first three steps of the Natural Roll.
(2) The Reverse Left Basic (bringing partner into a close hold).

This fig. may be followed by:
(1) The Reverse Left Basic.
(2) The first three steps of the Reverse Roll into the Natural Roll.

The Whisk

Note. Commencing to L. means moving towards the L.

GENTLEMAN

Commencing the Whisk to L., begin facing L.O.D. or the wall.

Whisk to L.
1. Side L.F. with a slight downward spring.   s.
2. Cross R.F. behind L.F.   "and"
3. Replace weight onto L.F. with slight downward spring.   s.

Whisk to R.
4. Side R.F. with slight downward spring.   s.
5. Cross L.F. behind R.F.   "and"
6. Replace weight onto R.F. with slight downward spring.   s.

LADY

Commencing the Whisk to L., begin backing L.O.D. or the wall.

Whisk to L.
1. Side R.F. with slight downward spring.   s.
2. Cross L.F. behind R.F.   "and"
3. Replace weight onto R.F. with slight downward spring.   s.

Whisk to R.
4. Side L.F. with slight downward spring.   s.
5. Cross R.F. behind L.F.   "and"
6. Replace weight onto L.F. with slight downward spring.   s.

Commencing the Whisk to L., this fig. may be preceded by:
(1) The first two steps of the Natural Right Basic (making no turn).
(2) A complete Reverse Left Basic (making no turn, or having turned to L. to face L.O.D. or the wall).

This fig. may be followed by:
(1) The Whisk to L. repeated.
(2) The Reverse Left Basic.
(3) The first three steps (Whisk to L. only) into Natural Right Basic, or the Quarter Turns (Progressive Movement).

Note. This fig. may be danced turning gradually to L. or progressing forwards.

The Whisk

Note. Commencing to R. means moving towards the R.

Commencing the Whisk to R., begin facing L.O.D. or the wall.

Whisk to R.	1. Side R.F. with slight downward spring.	s.
	2. Cross L.F. behind R.F.	"and"
	3. Replace weight onto R.F. with slight downward spring.	s.
Whisk to L.	4. Side L.F. with slight downward spring.	s.
	5. Cross R.F. behind L.F.	"and"
	6. Replace weight onto L.F. with slight downward spring.	s.

Commencing the Whisk to R., begin backing L.O.D. or the wall.

Whisk to R.	1. Side L.F. with slight downward spring.	s.
	2. Cross R.F. behind L.F.	"and"
	3. Replace weight onto L.F. with slight downward spring.	s.
Whisk to L.	4. Side R.F. with slight downward spring.	s.
	5. Cross L.F. behind R.F.	"and"
	6. Replace weight onto R.F. with slight downward spring.	s.

Commencing the Whisk to R., this fig. may be preceded by:
(1) The first two steps of the Reverse Left Basic.
(2) A complete Natural Right Basic.

This fig. may be followed by:
(1) The Whisk to R. repeated.
(2) The first three steps of the Whisk to R. into Reverse Left Basic.
(3) The Natural Right Basic.

Note. This fig. may be danced turning gradually to R. or progressing forwards.

Corta Jaca

This fig. is danced sideways onto the L.O.D., facing the wall.

1. Forward R.F., leading lady with a slight push of the arms.	s.
2. Forward L.F. onto the heel, keeping knees close.	Q.
3. Close R.F. towards L.F., on flat of foot.	Q.
4. Back L.F. onto the toe, keeping knees close.	Q.
5. Close R.F. towards L.F., on flat of foot.	Q.

Repeat 2, 3, 4 and 5 *ad lib.* and end with 2 and 3.

Corta Jaca

LADY

This fig. is danced sideways onto the L.O.D., backing the wall.

1. Back L.F., keeping arms firm for the lead.   s.
2. Back R.F. onto the toe, keeping knees close.   Q.
3. Close L.F. towards R.F., on flat of foot.   Q.
4. Forward R.F. onto the heel, keeping knees close.   Q.
5. Close L.F. towards R.F., on flat of foot.   Q.

Repeat 2, 3, 4 and 5 *ad lib.* and end with 2 and 3.

This fig. may be preceded by:
(1) The Natural Right Basic.
(2) The Quarter Turns (Progressive Movement).
(3) The change from Reverse Left Basic (1 and 2 of Reverse Left Basic).

This fig. may be followed by:
(1) The best ending to the Corta Jaca is to finish it by dancing 2 and 3 of it again and then step back on the L.F. (lady forward on R.F.) into 3 and 4 of the Natural Right Basic.

The Rocks

GENTLEMAN

Begin facing L.O.D. and finish facing L.O.D.

1. Forward R.F. (firm step).   s.
2. Forward L.F.   Q.
3. Slide R.F. slightly forward.   Q.
4. Slide L.F. forward.   s.
5. Forward R.F.   Q.
6. Slide L.F. slightly forward.   Q.
7. Slide R.F. forward.   s.

Repeat these seven steps once or twice.

This fig. may be preceded by:
(1) The Natural Right Basic danced to face L.O.D.
(2) First two steps of Left Reverse Basic (the change from Reverse to Natural Basic) danced facing L.O.D.

This fig. may be followed by:
(1) Making the seventh step the first step of the Natural Right Basic.
(2) Reverse Left Basic, only repeat the Rocks as far as the fourth step, making it the first step of the Reverse Left Basic.

The Rocks

LADY

Begin and finish backing L.O.D.

1. Back L.F.	s.
2. Place R. toe behind L. heel (toe turned out, knees close).	Q.
3. Slide L.F. to R. toe.	Q.
4. Move R.F. slightly back (toe straight).	s.
5. Place L. toe behind R. heel (toe turned out, knees close).	Q.
6. Slide R.F. to L. toe.	Q.
7. Move L.F. slightly back.	s.

Repeat these seven steps once or twice.

For preceding and following figs., see below the description of gentleman's steps.

The Volta

(*From Samba Whisks*)

GENTLEMAN

Dance 1 and 2 of the Natural Right Basic, followed by the Whisk to L. and the Whisk to R., ending with weight on R.F.

1. Place L. heel to R. toe, turning to L.	s.
2. Move R.F. slightly to R.	"and"
3. Draw L. heel to R. toe, turning to L.	s.
4. Move R.F. slightly to R.	"and"
5. Draw L. heel to R. toe, turning to L.	s.
6. Move R.F. slightly to R.	"and"
7. Draw L. heel to R. toe, turning to L.	s.

Dance the Whisk to R. and the Whisk to L., ending with weight on L.F., and follow with the Volta, turning to R.

1. Draw R. heel to L. toe, turning to R.	s.
2. Move L.F. slightly to L.	"and"
3. Draw R. heel to L. toe, turning to R.	s.
4. Move L.F. slightly to L.	"and"
5. Draw R. heel to L. toe, turning to R.	s.
6. Move L.F. slightly to L.	"and"
7. Draw R. heel to L. toe, turning to right.	s.

Dance the Whisk to L. and follow with the Natural Right Basic.

LADY

Dances normal opposite movements.

Samba Walk

GENTLEMAN

1. Forward R.F. in P.P. without weight, hips forward, knee relaxed.   s.
2. Pull hips back slightly, straightening R. knee, taking weight onto R.F.   s.
3. Forward L.F., in P.P., without weight, hips forward, knee relaxed.   s.
4. Pull hips back slightly, straightening L. knee, taking weight onto L.F.   s.

Repeat these four steps once or twice.

LADY

Dances the normal opposite movements.

This fig. may be preceded by:
(1) 1 and 2 of the Reverse Left Basic, opening partner to P.P.
(2) The Boto Fogo.

This fig. may be followed by:
(1) The Whisk after the fourth step; having turned to face lady, Whisk to R.
(2) The Volta after the second step (moving L. heel to R. toe, etc.).

Boto Fogo

GENTLEMAN

Begin facing wall.
1. Forward L.F.   s.
2. Side R.F., short step, turning slightly to L. ($\frac{1}{8}$ turn).   "and"
3. Replace weight onto L.F.   s.
4. Cross R.F. over L.F., O.P.   s.
5. Side L.F., short step, turning slightly to R. ($\frac{1}{4}$ turn).   "and"
6. Replace weight onto R.F.   s.
7. Cross L.F. over R.F., O.P.   s.
8. Side R.F., short step, turning to L. ($\frac{1}{4}$ turn).   "and"
9. Replace weight onto L.F.   s.

Repeat 4, 5, 6, 7, 8 and 9.

LADY

Begin backing wall.
1. Back R.F.   s.
2. Side L.F., short step, turning to R. ($\frac{1}{8}$ turn).   "and"
3. Replace weight on R.F.   s.
4. Cross L.F. over R.F., P.O.   s.

5. Side R.F., short step, turning to L. ($\frac{1}{4}$ turn).   "and"
6. Replace weight on L.F.   s.
7. Cross R.F. over L.F., P.O.   s.
8. Side L.F., short step, turning to R. ($\frac{1}{4}$ turn).   "and"
9. Replace weight on R.F.   s.

Repeat 4, 5, 6, 7, 8 and 9.

This fig. may be preceded by: | *This fig. may be followed by:*
(1) The Reverse Left Basic, facing wall. | (1) The Samba Walk, stepping forward with R.F. (lady L.F.) in P.P.

Progressive Boto Fogo

GENTLEMAN

Dances the Boto Fogo as before, but on step 3, instead of turning lady to P.P., he leads her to turn to her L. (so as to step back on her L.F.).

LADY

1. Back R.F.   s.
2. Side L.F., short step, turning to L. ($\frac{1}{8}$ turn).   "and"
3. Replace weight on R.F.   s.
4. Back L.F across body, P.O.   s.
5. Side R.F., short step, turning to R. ($\frac{1}{4}$ turn).   "and"
6. Replace weight on L.F.   s.
7. Cross R.F. behind L.F., P.O.   s.
8. Side L.F., short step, turning to L. ($\frac{1}{4}$ turn).   "and"
9. Replace weight on R.F.   s.

Repeat these nine steps once or twice, progressing down the L.O.D., ending with step 4 (gentleman, R.F. crossed over L.F.; lady, back L.F. across body). Close L.F. to R.F. (lady R.F. to L.F.) (s.).

This fig. may be preceded by: | *This fig. may be followed by:*
(1) The Reverse Left Basic. | (1) 3 and 4 of the Natural Right Basic (gentleman, back L.F., close R.F. to L.F.; lady, normal opposite but O.P.) into the Natural Right Basic.

CHAPTER XII

THE VIENNESE WALTZ (CONTINENTAL VERSION)

QUICK Waltzes are always popular and the Viennese Waltz appeals to those who do not care for Old Time dancing. The ideal tempo is fifty-two bars to the minute, but the figures may be danced to any waltz played between forty-four and sixty bars per minute. Figures 1, 2, 3 and 4 are the only figures necessary for enjoying dancing to this rhythm, and the two Fleckerl figures should only be used by advanced dancers.

Natural Right Turn

GENTLEMAN

Begin facing diag. to centre and finish facing diag. to centre.

1. Forward R.F., strong step. ⎫ Turning to R. to
2. Side L.F., long step. ⎬ backing diag. to
3. Close R.F. to L.F. ⎭ centre.
4. Back L.F., slightly to side.
5. Side R.F., short step.
6. Close L.F. to R.F., slightly back.

Amount of turn: Make ⅜ turn to R. between 1 and 2; make ⅛ turn to R. between 2 and 3; make ⅛ turn to R. between 3 and 4; make ⅜ turn to R. between 4 and 5.

Footwork: 1. H.T. 2. T. 3. T.H. 4. T.H. 5. T. 6. Foot flat.

Body sway: Sway slightly to L. on 1, changing to R. on 3; sway slightly to R. on 4, changing to L. on 6.

LADY

Dances gentleman's 4, 5, 6   1, 2, 3.

This fig. may be preceded by:
(1) The Forward Change Reverse to Natural.
(2) The Natural Turn.
(3) The Natural Fleckerl.

This fig. may be followed by:
(1) The Natural Turn.
(2) The Forward Change Natural to Reverse.
(3) The Natural Fleckerl.

Note. Travelling round the ballroom (on the outside), dance eight or sixteen bars of the Natural Turns before changing to another fig.

Reverse Turn

GENTLEMAN

Begin facing L.O.D. and finish facing L.O.D.

1. Forward L.F., strong step. ⎫ Turning to L.
2. Side R.F., long step. ⎬ to   backing
3. Cross L.F. in front of R.F. ⎭ L.O.D.
4. Back R.F., slightly to side.
5. Side L.F., short step.
6. Close R.F. to L.F., slightly back.

Amount of turn: Make $\frac{1}{4}$ turn to L. between 1 and 2; make $\frac{1}{4}$ turn to L. between 2 and 3; make $\frac{1}{8}$ turn to L. between 3 and 4; make nearly $\frac{3}{8}$ turn to L. between 4 and 5. Complete the turn between 5 and 6.

Footwork: 1. H.T.   2. T.   3. T.H.   4. T.H.   5. T.   6. Foot flat.
Body sway: Sway to L. on 2 and 3; sway to R. on 5 and 6.

LADY

Dances gentleman's 4, 5, 6   1, 2, 3.

This fig. may be preceded by:
(1) The Reverse Turn.
(2) The Forward Change from the Natural to Reverse.
(3) The Reverse Fleckerl.

This fig. may be followed by:
(1) The Reverse Turn.
(2) The Forward Change from the Reverse to Natural.
(3) The Reverse Fleckerl.

Note. Travelling round the ballroom, dance eight or sixteen bars of the Reverse Turns before changing to another fig.

Forward Change

Natural to Reverse

GENTLEMAN

Begin facing diag. to centre and finish facing L.O.D.

1. Forward R.F.
2. Side L.F., slightly forward.
3. Close R.F. to L.F.

Amount of turn: Make $\frac{1}{8}$ turn to R. between 1 and 2.
Footwork: 1. H.T.   2. T.   3. T.H.
Body sway: Sway to R. on 2 and 3.

LADY

Dances normal opposite movements.

This fig. may be preceded by:
(1) The Natural Turn.

This fig. may be followed by:
(1) The Reverse Turn.

Forward Change (Reverse to Natural)

GENTLEMAN

Begin facing L.O.D. and finish facing diag. to centre.

1. Forward L.F.
2. Side R.F., slightly forward.
3. Close L.F. to R.F.

Amount of turn: Make ⅛ turn to L. between 1 and 2.
Footwork: 1. H.T.   2. T.   3. T.H.
Body sway: Sway to L. on 2 and 3.

LADY

Dances normal opposite movements.

This fig. may be preceded by: *This fig. may be followed by:*
(1) The Reverse Turn.   (1) The Natural Turn.

Note. Changes from Natural to Reverse, and vice versa, should be
made on the musical phrasing. Do not change in the middle
of an eight-bar phrase, always change at the end, or continue
one of the turns and change at the end of the sixteen-bar phrase.

Natural Fleckerl

GENTLEMAN

Begin facing L.O.D. and finish facing L.O.D.

1. Diag. forward R.F. (facing diag. to wall).
2. Side L.F., half weight on it (backing L.O.D.).
3. Turn to R. on R.F. (facing L.O.D.).
4. Side L.F. (facing L.O.D.).
5. Cross R.F. well behind L.F., turn to R., weight still over L.F. (backing L.O.D.).
6. Turn to R. on L.F., uncrossing the feet (facing L.O.D.).

Amount of turn: Make ⅛ turn to R. on 1; make ⅛ turn to R. between
1 and 2; make ½ turn to R. between 2 and 3. No turn on 4. Make
½ turn to R. between 4 and 5; make ½ turn to R. between 5 and 6.
Footwork: 1. H.T.   2. T.   3. T.H.   4. H.T.   5. T.   6. T.H.
Body sway: Nil.

LADY

Dances gentleman's 4, 5, 6   1, 2, 3.

Note. The Fleckerl is a fast turn on one spot. Partner is held firmly
and in a close hold. When dancing the Natural Fleckerl, dance
Natural Turns to the centre of the room, and dance eight or sixteen
bars of Natural Fleckerls, then dance to the outside of the ballroom again with Natural Turns.

Reverse Fleckerl

GENTLEMAN

Begin facing L.O.D. and finish facing L.O.D.

1. Turn to L. on L. heel (pointing to centre).
2. Swing R.F. round, ending R.F. to side (backing L.O.D.).
3. Turn on R.F. to L. and cross L.F. loosely in front of R.F. (facing L.O.D.).
4. Side R.F., slightly back (backing diag. to wall against L.O.D.).
5. Cross L.F. well behind R.F. and turn to R. with weight on R.F. (backing L.O.D.).
6. Turn on R.F. to R. uncrossing the feet (facing L.O.D.), "and" change weight onto L.F.

Amount of turn: Make $\frac{1}{4}$ turn to L. on 1; make $\frac{1}{4}$ turn to L. between 1 and 2; make $\frac{1}{2}$ turn to L. between 2 and 3; make $\frac{1}{8}$ turn to L. between 3 and 4; make $\frac{3}{8}$ turn to L. between 4 and 5; make $\frac{1}{2}$ turn to L. between 5 and 6.

Footwork: 1. H.T. 2. T. 3. T.H. 4. T.H.T. 5. T. 6. T.H. of R.F., "and", H. of L.F.

Body sway: Nil.

LADY

Dances gentleman's 4, 5, 6   1, 2, 3.

Note. The Fleckerl is a fast turn on one spot. When dancing the Reverse Fleckerl, dance Reverse Turns to the centre of the ballroom, and dance eight or sixteen bars of Reverse Fleckerl, then dance Reverse Turns to the outside of the ballroom again.

A REMINDER

THE TECHNIQUE GIVEN IN THIS BOOK
UNDER THE DESCRIPTION OF EACH
FIGURE IS THAT WHICH IS USED BY
EVERY GOOD DANCER

Do not forget that the diagrams showing the positions of the feet in the different dances are not intended to be mathematically exact, but merely to show the pattern made in the various figures.

For full details of the abbreviations and explanations see pages 16–19.

By *Victor Silvester*

OLD TIME DANCING

The fundamental principles upon which both Old Time dances and the Twentieth Century Sequence dances are based are explained in non-technical language, and the result is a book of the utmost value to both beginners and keen competition dancers.

Illustrated   6s. net

MORE OLD TIME DANCES

To this further, up-to-the-minute volume of Old Time dances Silvester applies his simplified method of teaching, demonstrated in his previous books. For the novice he shows the simplest steps to hours of dancing enjoyment. For the more expert, the way to rapid improvement.

Illustrated   6s. net

SEQUENCE DANCING

In this book every dance is broken up into simple figures, each of a few easy steps, which anybody can learn in a matter of minutes. Instead of imparting theory, Silvester gets the reader dancing from the start.

Illustrated   6s. net

HERBERT JENKINS LTD., 3 Duke of York St., S.W.1.

THEORY AND TECHNIQUE
OF BALLROOM DANCING

by VICTOR SILVESTER

This book covers everything that is essential in connection with Ballroom Dancing, from a detailed description of the standardised figures—those that do not change—down to the finer points which go to the making of a good dancer. A large part of the book is devoted to Questions and Answers for a Ballroom Examination, and under this heading is given a complete analysis of the fundamental principles—everything that it is necessary to know, not only from the viewpoint of the experienced performer but from that of the biginner. 7*s*. 6*d*. net

OLD TIME DANCERS' HANDBOOK

by F. J. MAINEY

Dance News: " Altogether, a new kind of dance book. It contains controversy, research material, and plenty of dance descriptions, all well blended.

Crinoline: " *The* dance book of 1953. All Old Time Dancers need a good Old Time Handbook, and this one will answer a large number of the questions and problems which arise from time to time. 6*s*. net

HERBERT JENKINS LTD., 3 Duke of York St., S.W.1.